GEOGRAPHY, ENVIRONMENT, AND AMERICAN LAW

GEOGRAPHY, ENVIRONMENT, AND AMERICAN LAW

GARY L. THOMPSON, FRED M. SHELLEY, AND
CHAND WIJE, EDITORS

UNIVERSITY PRESS OF COLORADO

© 1997 by the University Press of Colorado

Published by the University Press of Colorado
P.O. Box 849
Niwot, Colorado 80544
(303) 530-5337

The University Press of Colorado is a cooperative publishing enterprise, supported,
in part, by Adams State College, Colorado State University, Fort Lewis College,
Mesa State College, Metropolitan State College of Denver, University of Colorado,
University of Northern Colorado, University of Southern Colorado,
and Western State College of Colorado.

The paper used in this publication meets the minimum standard requirements of the
National Standard for Information Sciences—Permanence of Paper for Printed
Library Materials. ANSI Z39.48—1984

Library of Congress Cataloging-in-Publication Data

Geography, environment, and American law / Gary L. Thompson,
Fred M. Shelley, and Chand Wije, editors.
    p. cm.
Includes index.
ISBN 0-87081-430-3 (casebound)
    1. Environmental law—United States. 2. Land use—Law and legislation—
United States. 3. Human geography. 4. Environmental sciences.
I. Thompson, Gary L., 1938– . II. Shelley, Fred M., 1952– . III. Wije, Chand,
1945– .
KF3775.G456 1997
344.73'046—dc20
[347.30446]

                                                          96-27504
                                                          CIP

10 9 8 7 6 5 4 3 2 1

CONTENTS

CONTRIBUTORS

Gary L. Thompson is associate professor of the department of geography at the University of Oklahoma.

Fred M. Shelley is associate professor of geography and planning at Southwest Texas State University.

Chand Wije is an environmental consultant in Austin, Texas.

Risa Palm is dean of the College of Arts and Sciences at the University of Oregon.

W. Wesley Pue is Nemetz Professor of Legal History at the University of British Columbia.

James N. Corbridge Jr. is professor of law at the University of Colorado.

Otis W. Templer is professor of geography at Texas Tech University.

Rutherford H. Platt is professor of geography at the University of Massachusetts, Amherst.

Olen Paul Matthews is professor and chair of the department of geography at the University of New Mexico.

Ernest S. Easterly III is professor of law at Southern University.

Jeroen Wagendorp is water resource specialist for the Barry County Health Department in Hastings, Michigan, and adjunct professor of geography at Western Michigan University.

PREFACE

During the 1980s, Gary Thompson, Chand Wije, and I were members of the Department of Geography at the University of Oklahoma. Over the years, we frequently talked about various aspects of the relationships between geography and law, with particular interest in environmental law in the United States. In discussing these issues, we soon became aware that very little literature has explored the relationships between geography and environmental law in the United States.

Although geographers and lawyers often address similar issues, there has been minimal interface between their respective disciplines. This is particularly true in the area of environmental issues. A substantial literature relating law and human geography has developed in recent years. This has not been matched by comparable interaction between law and environmental geography despite the historic role of environmental issues in the discipline of geography and despite the increasing importance of environmental issues in American society. We are hopeful that this book will provide an initial impetus toward the establishment of a research agenda that links the two fields more directly.

The lack of interface between geography and environmental law stems, in part, from the fact that the two fields approach similar research problems from very different intellectual perspectives. Although geographers are concerned with the description of the unique characteristics of places, many are also anxious to understand relationships between processes and patterns. Environmental geographers focus particularly on problems of human beings in the natural world. How do people cope with natural hazards and natural disasters? How do they identify, use, and value natural resources? How has modern technology contributed to climatic change, and how might any resulting changes in climate in turn affect settlement, agriculture, water use, and other aspects of society? These are but a few of the questions addressed in recent geographical literature involving the interface between society and the natural world.

Law approaches these and similar problems from a different yet complementary perspective. While geographers seek spatial regularity, lawyers seek solutions to particular problems. The American legal tradition, like the English common-law tradition upon which American law is based, emphasizes the role of precedent. Legal disputes are decided not only on the basis of laws themselves, but also with reference to centuries of previous cases involving similar or analogous situations. Thus, the lawyer is less concerned with the development of general principles, and more with the application of principles to particular situations.

As the chapters in this volume illustrate, law and environmental geography can be approached in several ways. Laws create geography; that is, differences in laws contribute to differences between places. Differences in laws concerning air- or water-quality standards, for example, result in differences in industrial structure or environmental quality. At the same time, laws are the product of geography. Many laws are not written or applied uniformly; rather, they are modified in accordance with local conditions. Thus, California, whose large population is concentrated in basins subject to atmospheric inversions and hence to air pollution, has enacted stricter air pollution controls than many other states. Similarly, water law principles vary across the country. The riparian principle derived from English common law and used as the basis of water law in the humid eastern states is replaced in the arid West by the appropriate principle.

This volume, with contributions by distinguished scholars in both geography and law, provides an interesting variety of complementary perspectives on the increasingly important interface between geography and environmental law in the United States. We hope that it will provide a springboard for creation of a research agenda through which scholars in both fields can identify and explore common ground and help to provide creative, meaningful solutions to the major environmental problems currently facing the United States.

We wish to acknowledge the valuable assistance of officials at the University Press of Colorado in expediting the completion of this project. Jody Berman, who oversaw completion of this project, was unfailingly helpful, cooperative, and patient with us during the publication process. Alice Colwell did an outstanding job in copyediting the manuscript, particularly with the often confusing and difficult footnotes. We also appreciate the cooperation of the chapter authors, who likewise were patient during a period in which the editors faced a variety of challenging problems and career moves that slowed completion of the project. Finally, we wish to acknowledge the support of our families during the publication process.

Fred M. Shelley

GEOGRAPHY, ENVIRONMENT,
AND AMERICAN LAW

INTRODUCTION

GARY L. THOMPSON, FRED M. SHELLEY, AND CHAND WIJE

This volume explores the commonalities and complementarities of two important intellectual traditions: geography and the study of American law. With respect to environmental concerns, the intellectual content of these disciplines links them to each other, but over the past century both have evolved in divergent directions. Current environmental problems and crises mandate increasing mutual familiarity and interdependence between the two streams of scholarship. This collection tries to illustrate and motivate efforts to apply the interpretive and analytic skills of professional geographers to environmental issues by examining the roles that geographers and legal scholars have played in understanding and resolving problems associated with land use, water resources, mineral development, and related environmental issues. It is hoped that this volume will enable legal scholars and other professionals to envision the promise and prospect of geography as a useful frame for analyzing complex human–environmental challenges.

Contemporary geography is concerned with explaining the location and distribution of physical and cultural phenomena on the earth's surface, the agencies and principles underlying such distributions, and how these distributions change over time. Geography is distinguished from other disciplines on the basis of scope, perspective, and method rather than content. None of the subjects professional geographers study is unique to geography; rather, what distinguishes the geographic approach from those of other disciplines is how the geographer conceptualizes his or her subject matter. The geographical approach emphasizes questions of where and why.

There are two main branches of geography: *physical geography,* which explores the dynamics of the earth's biological and physical systems, and *human geography,* which examines the character and effects that human activity has on the earth's surface. One major research tradition of geography addresses the interaction between human activity and the environment, thus spanning the human-physical dualism. Evidence that human activity influences climate, air and water quality, stream flow, and many other aspects of the earth's systems is well known. Many human geographers devote their research energies to understanding the dynamics and significance of such impacts on the earth's physical environments.

Conversely, the effects of dynamic, natural systems on human activity are also of great interest to geographers. Both research interests link social and natural sciences: Environmental degradation and catastrophe are matters of politics and economics, not merely science and technology.

Since the 1960s, human geographers and other social scientists have begun to appreciate the importance of law in human activity. At the same time, legal scholars, lawyers, judges, and legislators have become more and more reliant on the scientific community for information concerning social and natural processes and their effects on human life and environmental quality. The 1990s have witnessed an upsurge in human geographers' interest in the law and the roles geographers play in the legal system. An increasing number of respected professional geographers, many of whom have completed formal training in the law, have contributed to this understanding.[1] The chapters in this volume contribute to this genre of literature by focusing explicitly on issues involving land use and environmental law.

GEOGRAPHY, ENVIRONMENT, AND AMERICAN LAW THROUGH HISTORY

The relationships among geography, environment, and law have evolved over nearly four centuries of Anglo-American settlement of the North American continent. For most of American history, the primary concern of Americans was the occupation, settlement, and development of the vast land resource base of the United States. American law was geared toward expediting the divestment of land and the development of resources. By the end of the nineteenth century, however, the pattern of Anglo-American settlement in North America had been established. No longer could Americans regard the resources of the United States as unlimited. Gradually, American legal institutions adjusted to fit the reality of limited resources. By the late twentieth century, mounting evidence of local, regional, and worldwide environmental deterioration had stimulated the further development of American environmental law.

Although many nationalities contributed to the European settlement of North America, the thirteen colonies that would become the United States were under the formal political control of Britain, and settlement was dominated by migrants from the British Isles. British settlers brought English legal institutions with them across the Atlantic, and these legal traditions formed the cornerstone of Anglo-American law, which remains one of the world's major legal traditions.[2]

Anglo-American law is based on the principle of common law, which — in contrast to the civil law tradition of the Roman Empire and continental Europe — emphasizes evolving values and attitudes of the population, paying considerable attention to local customs. Common law is "judge-made law — molded, refined, examined, and changed in the crucible of action and handed down from generation to generation in the form of reported cases."[3] Thus the highest expression of common law is not a written code but evolving precedent.

The two sources of law in the Anglo-American legal tradition are statutes and previous cases. Courts have the responsibility of interpreting the meaning and applicability of statutes enacted by Congress and the state legislatures as well as interpreting and applying previous cases to analogous situations. In adjudicating disputes, judges rely on previously decided cases that deal with similar issues or problems, ensuring continuity in the application of law over time. Differences in the facts of a case in question from the situations covered in precedent cases means that the judicial role requires the interpretation, not merely the application, of the law.

Through the course of American history, the legal system evolved constantly in accordance with major changes in the American political economy. Even before the American Revolution, law had changed considerably to fit the geographical circumstances associated with the settlement of a vast, sparsely inhabited continent. After the achievement of independence, American law and legal traditions continued to evolve as the country matured from an agricultural and mining frontier to a complex industrial society and beyond.

Eighteenth-century British law remained "unwritten"; in contrast to modern American law, it lacked a foundation in a written constitution. The idea that the lawmaking authority of government needed grounding in a written constitution began to take shape shortly before the Revolution. To a considerable extent, sentiment of the period reflected the belief that American colonists received inequitable treatment by the British government. Yet the legality of the Stamp Act, the Proclamation of 1763, and other offensive actions of Parliament stood unquestioned. In response, American patriots "concluded that Parliament was not the embodiment of sovereign authority and that the fundamental principles of government had to be in writing if they were to have meaning."[4] The principles of governance had to be separated from the products of its actions.

After the Revolution, Americans formalized this separation by establishing a written constitution. The U.S. Constitution remains the framework for U.S. law. During the first century of American independence, American law developed into a full-fledged, legal tradition independent of although not entirely separate from its British antecedents. The Constitution established on paper the basic institutions of American law, and after the document's ratification these institutions came into common use, with considerable trial and error.

During the nineteenth century, European settlement spilled across the Appalachians, the plains, and the Rockies to the Pacific coast. Law played a very important role in the distribution of land and the development of America's variegated natural resource base. Federal and state law encouraged and regulated the rapid diffusion of immigrants and the exploitation of soils, forests, minerals, and biotic resources. The law promoted private ownership and enterprise, and governments built roads, canals, and bridges. These and other infrastructural improvements underpinned efforts to promote economic growth in the fledgling republic. For example, the state of New York invested more than $7 million in the construction of the Erie Canal, which within a short time became a major commercial artery. By the end of the nineteenth century, in order to encourage the extension of rail lines, Congress had granted to various railroad companies land equivalent in area to that of the state of Texas.[5]

Particular attention was paid to the transfer of public lands to private ownership. A primary motive of public land divestment during the nineteenth century was to realize the Jeffersonian vision of a country made up of independent, freeholding small families. The Homestead Act of 1862 and other laws institutionalized public and private goals of promoting settlement and land improvement.

In 1890 the U.S. census described the American frontier as largely closed — a development that coincided with the publication of Frederick Jackson Turner's famous essay on the significance of the frontier in American history.[6] No longer could ordinary Americans expect to settle previously unused lands. Industrialization challenged the blueprint of rural life, and growth within the American polity began the shift toward urban centers. The urban shift profoundly affected the dimensions of American law and legal institutions.

During the nineteenth century, American law allocated and distributed wealth in the form of resources. A primary concern became the orderly distribution of land for the maximum benefit of a growing population. Toward the end of that century, Americans increasingly began to realize the limits of their land and resource base. Accordingly, American law became less concerned with distribution and more concerned with regulation. The shift of emphasis from distribution to regulation coincided with widespread concern about the abuse and disappearance of forestlands, the Populist movement of the 1890s, and the Progressive reforms of the early twentieth century. Government increasingly accepted the responsibility of regulating the economy in order to protect the rights of all individuals, urban and rural. By the 1970s the shift in law and policy had begun to encompass the *protection* of the physical environmental systems rather than the divestment and development of all available lands and waters.

A brief examination of the development of twentieth-century land use and environmental law illustrates the magnitude of this fundamental change in legal philosophy. During the first century of American independence, American land law was based on the premise that land was a commodity, that real property could be bought and sold freely and used or "enjoyed" as only the owner saw fit. The notion of governmental interference as an anathema to the enjoyment of private property had become deeply entrenched in the law and the American mind. Further, many nineteenth-century Americans chose to regard public lands as an almost inexhaustible resource.

Despite the sacred status of private property, Americans took steps to protect scarce and unusual types of land. In 1872 Congress set aside Yellowstone National Park and established the national park system, charging the National Park Service with administering public lands "for the benefit and enjoyment of the people." Two decades later, Congress empowered the president to proclaim additional lands as public reservations. Many Progressives, led by Theodore Roosevelt, lent wholehearted support to the burgeoning conservation movement, which was devoted to promoting the more efficient development of the nation's now limited resource base through scientific management policies.

The conservation movement spearheaded efforts to develop national parks, protect forests, and improve the management of scarce and spectacular land and natural resources. The Department of the Interior, the Bureau of Reclamation, and other agencies were established during this period to assist in the regulatory process, while the U.S. Army Corps of Engineers and the Tennessee Valley Authority were empowered to use technical expertise to improve the efficiency of resource development. But what of ordinary agricultural, residential, industrial, and commercial land? Did government have the right to regulate its use?

During the early twentieth century, state and local governments began to enact comprehensive land use and zoning laws. The Supreme Court upheld the constitutionality of land use zoning in *Village of Euclid* v. *Ambler Realty Co.*[7] Land use zoning was justified as an extension of nuisance law, which is based on the principle that the owner of property whose value suffers because of the activities of others is entitled to compensation. Yet the public interest justified the right of government to regulate various uses on private lands. As several of the chapters in this volume indicate, contemporary land use and environmental law require balancing the competing claims of the public interest against the right of the property owner to determine the use of his or her land.

Although *Euclid* established the government's right to regulate land use, disputes concerning land use policy intensified throughout the twentieth century. Naturally, many such disputes revolved around the question of what constituted the public interest. Landowners whose profits were affected by regulation sued to overturn or mitigate these rules. Other cases involved questions of liability. Who is responsible for compensating victims of environmental degradation? As scientists became increasingly aware of the complexity and interconnectedness of the earth's ecosystem, the question of liability became more and more complicated. Assignment of liability and calculation of damages to the natural environment proved much more difficult to determine than damages paid to a specific individual.

Nevertheless, the late twentieth century has witnessed a revolution in land use and environmental law. By the 1960s scientific knowledge of ecology and of the impacts of human activity on the earth's physical environment had grown dramatically. As America's industrial base continued to expand, air and water pollution increased, and the American public became aware of the dangers associated with environmental degradation.[8] Many Americans came to regard undeveloped land as valuable rather than wasted, and they participated in a growing environmental movement with steadily mounting influence in American politics. The first Earth Day, on April 22, 1970, came to symbolize the growing strength of environmentalism.

The environmental movement of the late twentieth century differs remarkably from the conservation movement of the early 1900s. Rachel Carson's *Silent Spring* began a value-laden paradigm shift in attitudes toward the environment. Earlier *conservationists* were dedicated to using science and technology to bring about the more efficient and less wasteful development of the nation's natural resource base, whereas *environmentalists* argue the need for government action to promote and protect environmental quality for its own sake.[9] Achievement of this objective often required that land and natural resources be protected from development in order to preserve them, and scientific evidence concerning the effects of human activity on the ecology of various natural environments supports such legislation and litigation.

Since the 1960s both the federal government and the states have enacted a wide variety of environmental protection statutes. The Clean Air Act of 1963, the Wild and Scenic Rivers Act of 1968, the Federal Water Pollution Control Act of 1972, the Resource Conservation and Recovery Act of 1976, the Clean Water Act of 1977, and the Hazardous and Solid Waste Amendments of 1984 are but a few of the many federal initiatives signed into law over the past three decades. Environmental responsibilities of existing federal agencies such as the Department of the Interior were expanded, while new agencies such as the Department of Energy and the Environmental Protection Agency were created. Similar agencies established in many states (as in Michigan, described in Chapter 8) were charged with administering and enforcing federal and state environmental laws.

The very success of the environmental movement in securing passage of environmental protection laws and regulations generated renewed controversy. The older conservation ethic and the new environmental movement represented fundamentally conflicting sets of values, which clashed intensely as American economic growth rates began to falter in the economic chaos of the 1970s. In light of the recession of the 1970s, many questioned whether environmental protection was hindering the possibility of economic development, particularly in the country's interior. In response to the energy crises of the 1970s, the administrations of Gerald Ford and Jimmy Carter pursued policies intended to expedite domestic fuel production and reduce American dependence on imported petroleum. The administration of Ronald Reagan in the 1980s actively opposed many environmental initiatives of the 1960s and 1970s, although as time wore on, it became evident that environmentalism was much more popular with the voting public than many Reagan policymakers realized. Today leaders of both major parties advertise their commitment to environmental quality, but the rhetoric of environmentalism has by no means been matched by legislative output sought by various proponents of the movement.

GEOGRAPHY AND ENVIRONMENTAL LAW

Many of the controversies involving environmental regulation and the competing objectives of environmental protection and economic growth ended up in federal and state courts. The judiciary was charged with developing and interpreting a growing body of law, much of which dealt with highly complex and scientifically sophisticated information. Law had to be applied to a wide variety of new situations, and in many cases it became clear that the law was inconsistent with scientific reality. Since the 1960s there have been greater efforts to base legal principles more directly on scientific knowledge.

Explosive development in the areas of environmental science and environmental law has created a need for geographical analysis and interpretation and a niche for physical and human geographers who are uniquely qualified to develop intellectual linkages between the scientific and legal communities. In light of the historical development of American environmental law, how can an understanding of geography contribute to the interpretation of the law in the future? The essays in this book identify two important ways. First, geographers can use their professional expertise to provide meaningful information to legal scholars, legislators, lawyers, and judges. Second, geographers are positioned to help show how and why laws and their societal consequences vary from place to place. Geography is the only science-based, scholarly discipline devoted to a holistic view of human-environmental interactions.

Over the course of the twentieth century, social science research has come to play an increasingly important role in legal matters. Although nineteenth-century lawyers and judges paid little attention to the research findings of scientists and social scientists, courts during the Progressive era of the early twentieth century began to take notice of studies by experts outside the legal profession. In *Muller* v. *Oregon* the Supreme Court used the findings of sociological research to uphold the constitutionality of an Oregon law that limited the length of the workday for female employees.[10] The sociologists whose research underlay the Court's decision in *Muller* believed that the law was justified because long workdays were deleterious to a woman's health and family relationships.

While contemporary Americans may find the arguments of *Muller* quaint and paternalistic, the case established the use of scientific research to provide factual information upon which to base legal rulings. Today the use of scientific information in legal proceedings is commonplace. Many professional geographers have served as expert witnesses; geographical expertise has contributed to a wide variety of decisions involving such issues as water management, natural hazards, mineral development, and transboundary disputes. In the future, geographers whose social science knowledge has been augmented by training in the physical and environmental sciences are likely to play increasingly important roles in the resolution of complex environmental disputes. Several of the chapters in this volume describe cases in which geographers' testimony has been critical to the outcome of litigation.

Geographers are also uniquely qualified to help in predicting and understanding the social and physical consequences of laws and court decisions. Many federal laws, for example, apply uniformly across the United States although their consequences for local populations may vary considerably. Laws appropriate to some areas are useless or dysfunctional in other geographical contexts. For example, the tendency for smog to form in basins in mountain regions means that large western cities, notably Los Angeles, Phoenix, and Denver, are particularly subject to smog. Air pollution and emissions standards are enforced more strictly in these areas by federal and state law. Thus California requires tighter emissions control standards for new and used vehicles than do other states — and as a result a new car costs somewhat more in California than elsewhere. To take another example, the cost of controlling freon gas emissions to protect atmospheric ozone falls heavily on areas that rely on air conditioning in summer months.

The relationship between law and geography is illustrated by spatial variation in American water law. British water law is based on the *riparian* principle, which grants ownership of water in streams, ponds, and other bodies of water to the owner of land adjacent to them. The riparian principle is useful in the eastern United States, which like the British Isles is blessed with abundant rainfall. Settlers crossing the Great Plains soon discovered that most of the western United States was arid country, where crops could not be grown without a consistent supply of water for irrigation. Only in those places where water could be obtained and developed was successful settlement possible. Americans west of the 100th meridian thus developed the principle of *prior appropriation,* which assigns the right to use water to the first person to identify and develop that water, regardless of location. Today the prior appropriation principle underlies the water law of most western states, whereas the riparian principle is the basis for water law east of the 100th meridian.

Since the 1960s geographic understanding of the dynamics of human interaction with the natural environment has increased dramatically. Worldwide concern about environmental problems with potentially devastating consequences such as global warming, tropical rainforest depletion, and desertification has spurred considerable research into the dynamics of the earth's physical systems and how these have been influenced or modified by human activities. Growing expertise in the dynamics of the global environment is paralleled by the development and application of computer-based geographic information systems, remote sensing, and mapping programs that have expedited the process of geographical analysis. Because their training and professional expertise links the social and natural sciences, geographers are in a position to understand the global environment and the relationships between human activity and the biosphere. It is certain that such knowledge will prove critical to the future development of environmental law, and it is hoped that government officials throughout the world will call on geographers to provide expertise to foster the development of wise, humane, and farsighted laws involving environmental issues.

OVERVIEW OF THE BOOK

The remaining chapters in this volume illustrate the interactive relationship between geography and environmental law in the United States. Chapters 1 and 2 deal specifically with the nature of contemporary geographic thought and its relationships with law and the legal system. In Chapter 1, Risa Palm provides an introduction to the nature and scope of the contemporary discipline of geography. Geographers study variability over space and time in the distribution of populations, cultures, customs, economic activities, land uses, and social and political patterns. Geographers are also concerned with the relationships between human settlement and culture and the physical environment. Both of these research traditions are useful to the development and application of the law. That legal structures often influence locational processes demonstrates the importance of a close working relationship between the disciplines of law and geography.

Palm illustrates that geographers working from the perspectives of location in space and interactions between society and the physical environment can contribute to legal issues in several ways. Geographers can map the distribution of users and providers of legal services; they can analyze the impacts of laws and legal organization; and they can investigate how law accelerates or hinders the impacts of social, economic, and political activity on the earth's physical system. Thus geographers are especially qualified to contribute to the development and analysis concerning environmental regulation and land use.

Palm then uses several contemporary examples to illustrate the potential of geographical knowledge for legal purposes. A case study of California's law requiring real estate agents to disclose the location of surface fault zones to prospective home buyers illustrates that the broad purpose of the law has not been fulfilled, because few homeowners use such information in making decisions concerning property purchase. A second study of growth control legislation in California illustrates that environmentally motivated legislation led to a steep rise in house prices, calling into question the possibility that the social and environmental objectives of the law could be satisfied simultaneously. These and other examples illustrate the extent to which both fields will be enhanced by closer cooperation.

In Chapter 2 lawyer and legal scholar W. Wesley Pue examines the issue of cooperation between law and geography from a lawyer's perspective. Pue's chapter provides a historical analysis of the intellectual development of legal studies over the past century. During the late nineteenth century, most law schools emphasized a highly positivistic approach to the study of law. The task of legal scholars was to seek the "correct" answer to a legal problem, irrespective of its political or economic consequences. The facts underlying particular disputes were to be combined with appropriate laws in order to render correct and noncontroversial decisions.

As we have seen, over the course of the twentieth century social science has become much more effectively integrated with law. Law is no longer regarded as merely a set of rules or codes but as an intellectual and ideological force that interacts with and influences many other spheres of intellectual and ideological endeavor. This revised approach to the study and analysis of law promotes a more effective integration of law and geography.

Pue identifies several avenues for integrating law and geography. Impact analysis, or study of the actual effects of law and legal principles on local communities, may prove a major contribution to a more meaningful exploration of linkages among law, geography, and the theory of the state. Thus Pue's arguments from a lawyer's perspective parallel Palm's analysis from a geographer's perspective.

Chapters 3 and 4 examine the complex and important topic of water law. As we have indicated, two legal theories underlie American water law. In Chapter 3, James N. Corbridge Jr. focuses on some of the geographical implications of water law in the United States. The development and application of water law are complicated by the increasing demands on available water supplies. Environmentalists and recreational users whose enjoyment of the watercourse demands that water be maintained in situ compete with farmers, industrialists, and other users who intend to withdraw water for use elsewhere. Corbridge reviews recent cases in which state courts have had to interpret these and other conflicts stemming from greater demand for scarce water.

In reviewing these cases, Corbridge illustrates the importance of the geographer's role in the application of water law. Geographical analysis of water use, management, and distribution would prove a useful step toward the development of more effective legislation in order to guide the courts in allocating scarce water resources. Geographers can also contribute to disputes between the states concerning their legal obligations to deliver water to downstream neighbors. For example, the Supreme Court has had to adjudicate conflict among Colorado, New Mexico, and Texas concerning the allocation of the waters of the Rio Grande. Similar conflicts have occurred on the Colorado, the Arkansas, and other major rivers that flow across state boundaries.

While Corbridge takes a national view, Otis W. Templer in Chapter 4 concentrates on water law in the state of Texas. The water law of Texas, whose physical environment ranges from the hot, rainy bottomlands of East Texas to the arid deserts of the El Paso region, is derived from both riparian and appropriation principles. In analyzing Texas water law from a geographical perspective, Templer contrasts the institutional framework of American water law with scientific understanding of water resources. Nature's hydrologic cycle explains the movement of water through the atmosphere, the earth's surface, the oceans, and underground. While scientists regard all of these components of the hydrologic cycle as interrelated, the law governing the use of water at each stage of the cycle varies widely. Water law often depends on the form in which the water is found, ignoring the hydrologic cycle. Thus the law governing surface water may have no relationship with that governing the use of groundwater or precipitation. In fact, many of the legal principles used to manage water resources in Texas, as elsewhere, were developed long before scientists had accurate knowledge of the processes of the hydrologic cycle.

Many experts agree that conjunctive management of water, linking the various aspects of the hydrologic cycle into a single legal system, may be desirable. Although conjunctive management has been tried with varying degrees of success in other western states, Templer is pessimistic that such a solution will be attempted in Texas in the immediate future. Nevertheless, Templer illustrates how geographers can contribute much to the analysis of water law by emphasizing the need to view water law and water rights within the framework of a totally integrated resource.

In Chapter 5 Rutherford H. Platt examines the role of judicial perception of geographical context as a basis for understanding the outcomes of land use decisions. Decision outcomes are often influenced by a judge's perception of their potential geographical consequences, underscoring the importance of geographical understanding to the legal process. Platt contrasts the adversarial approach of law with the deterministic orientation of geography. In land use controversies, for example, the law maintains a rigid definition of parties of interest to legal decisions, whereas geography's framework is more flexible and identifies potential parties of interest on the basis of a diverse and changing set of criteria. As Platt's analysis demonstrates, most major cases concerning land use that have been decided recently by the Supreme Court involve the issue of governmental authority to regulate private activities.

Public health, safety, and welfare must be balanced against potential injuries and costs suffered by landowners. Platt reviews several important cases involving mining, zoning, and other aspects of land use in order to illustrate the impacts of geography on contemporary American land use law.

Chapter 6, by Olen Paul Matthews, deals with legal problems associated with mining and mineral resource development. Those intent on mineral exploration must comply with numerous federal and state laws and regulations in order to minimize pollution and protect the nearby environment. The process of obtaining the permits needed to initiate a mining process may take up to five years.

In many areas mineral rights are owned separately from the land where the minerals are located. Matthews shows how American law concerning ownership of mineral rights has evolved since colonial times. Because much of the mineral potential of the contemporary United States is on federally owned land, a clear understanding of the federal system is critical to understanding mineral acquisition. In a flowchart illustrating the steps by which mining interests can obtain permits from the federal government, Matthews presents four different types of claims, each associated with different rights. Under certain circumstances mineral rights can also be leased or purchased. Matthews's discussion of the process of mineral exploration in the Cabinet Mountains wilderness area in northwestern Montana illustrates the complexity and controversy inherent in the permitting process.

In Chapter 7, Ernest S. Easterly III focuses on one important aspect of the geographer's contribution to law — the role of the geographer in providing information for the litigation process, in this case in helping to determine boundaries. Geographers are especially qualified to provide expert advice concerning the determination of marine boundaries, because marine boundary delineation statutes are seldom as precise or as specific as those delineating boundaries on land.

Easterly begins by describing procedures by which riparian and marine boundaries can be drawn in order to resolve conflicts concerning the precise location of a boundary. These methods may not always work, however, because of disagreement over the historic meanings of place-names and over the locations of features named in the documents identifying boundaries. Yet most such disputes can be settled in a satisfactory fashion if commonsense principles involving the preparation and interpretation of maps are followed.

Easterly uses a case study of a boundary dispute in Lake Pontchartrain, Louisiana, to illustrate the general principles outlined in the earlier part of his chapter. Disputes over boundaries between parishes (the Louisiana equivalent of counties) stem from the state's history of British, French, and

Spanish colonization. Representatives of several of the parishes that share jurisdiction over the waters of Lake Pontchartrain invited geographers to offer advice in a long-standing and costly boundary dispute. Such information was crucial to the interpretation of a Louisiana Supreme Court decision that identified "the middle" of Lake Pontchartrain as the boundary between parishes. After extensive debate, the Louisiana legislature adopted the solution advocated by the geographers.

Chapter 8, by Jeroen Wagendorp, presents a case study of the impacts of Michigan's environmental laws. The state of Michigan is characterized by substantial internal differences in environment, urbanization, economy, and political culture. The state can be divided into three broad regions: the Detroit metropolitan area and the southern part of the Lower Peninsula, the northern half of the Lower Peninsula, and the Upper Peninsula. The southern half of the Lower Peninsula contains the majority of Michigan's population and economic activity, while the economy of the northern part of the Lower Peninsula is dominated by agriculture and tourism. The social and physical infrastructure of the Upper Peninsula is poorly developed, its economy dominated by mining, logging, and tourism and its lack of development reinforced by isolation from the population centers of lower Michigan.

In the early 1970s, the Michigan legislature passed the Michigan Environmental Protection Act, a statute that explicitly authorized citizen-initiated environmental lawsuits. The act is administered by the Land and Water Management Division of the Michigan state government, which is responsible for the administration and enforcement of federal and state environmental programs. Citizens wishing to initiate environmental modification projects must obtain permits from the division. Wagendorp's analysis of the 6,515 permit applications reviewed by the division in 1987 indicated that the Upper Peninsula and northern lower Michigan are subject to the political objectives of the more populous and prosperous southern part of the state. Statewide environmental regulation fails to take the unique situation of the northern parts of the state into account. Wagendorp concludes that the economic dependency of the north on the south may be reinforced by the nature of Michigan's environmental law.

CONCLUSION

The nine chapters that follow present but a few of the interesting problems of contemporary significance that integrate the research traditions of geography, environment, and American law. As our scientific knowledge continues to expand and as the earth's physical system is increasingly affected by pollution and other by-products of human activity, we can expect even more concern on the part of the legal and scientific communities to integrate their intellectual approaches. Those in the field of geography have a unique opportunity to effect this integration, and it is hoped that more and more geographers will become involved in this research effort and that lawyers and legislators will thus become more aware of the contributions of geographers to understanding the influence of law on the relationships between society and environment. Geography remains the only discipline with a primary commitment to understanding the human-environmental problems that now proliferate at every level from the local community to the global polity.

NOTES

1.   Gordon L. Clark (1985), *Judges and the Cities* (Chicago: University of Chicago Press); Nicholas K. Blomley and Gordon L. Clark (1990), "Law, Theory and Geography," *Urban Geography,* 11, pp. 433–446; Nicholas K. Blomley (1994), *Law, Space and the Geographies of Power* (New York: Guilford Press).

2.   Ernest S. Easterly (1977), "Global Patterns of Legal Systems: Notes Toward a New Jurisprudence," *Geographical Review,* 67, pp. 209–220.

3.   Lawrence M. Friedman (1973), *A History of American Law.* New York: Simon and Schuster, p. 17.

4.   Kermit Hall (1989), *The Magic Mirror: Law in American History.* New York: Oxford University Press, p. 57.

5.   Ibid., p. 193.

6.   Frederick Jackson Turner (1893), "The Significance of the Frontier in American History," *Annual Report of the American Historical Association,* pp. 199–227.

7.   *Village of Euclid* v. *Ambler Realty Co.,* 272 U.S. 386 (1926).

8.   Stewart Udall (1963), *The Quiet Crisis* (New York: Holt, Rinehart and Winston); Rachel Carson (1962), *Silent Spring* (Boston: Houghton Mifflin).

9.   Samuel P. Hays (1989), *Beauty, Health and Permanence: Environmental Politics in the United States, 1955-1985.* New York: Cambridge University Press.

10.   *Muller* v. *Oregon,* 208 U.S. 412 (1908).

1
GEOGRAPHY AND ENVIRONMENTAL LAW
RISA PALM

WHAT IS GEOGRAPHY?

The roots of contemporary geography date back to ancient Greek scholarship. The word "geography" itself comes from two Greek words: "geo," meaning "the earth," and "graphein," meaning "to write." Thus the literal meaning of geographym is "writing about the earth." The distinguished American geographer Richard Hartshorne stated that "geography is concerned to provide accurate, orderly, and rational description and interpretation of the variable character of the earth surface."[1]

As Hartshorne's definition indicates, geographical thinking involves two components — description and interpretation. For centuries, the former dominated geographical thinking. The Greeks and other ancient and medieval peoples expressed keen interest in exploring, mapping, and describing the world around them. Travelers to previously unknown places returned with accounts of peoples and environments they had visited, providing the information various societies used to understand the world around them and the place of peoples within it.

By the end of the Middle Ages, European mariners began the systematic exploration of the earth's surface. Over the next several centuries, a wealth of information about places throughout the world accumulated. The earth's surface was mapped with greater and greater accuracy as more and more detailed information was amassed and catalogued.

The Age of Discovery came to an end at the close of the nineteenth century. By this time the task of describing previously unknown areas of the earth's surface had largely been completed. To be sure, description remains an important component of contemporary geographical thinking. Information gathered from satellites provides a more thorough understanding of the earth's landscape and changes in the character of the earth's surface. Yet most contemporary geography involves the interpretation of information about the earth's surface and its inhabitants. Interpretation has replaced description as the central focus of geography.

Contemporary geography includes two major branches. Physical geographers study climate, landforms, and biotic realms. Human geographers, in contrast, investigate the human occupance and use of the earth's surface; they are thus concerned with variability over space and time in the distribution of populations, cultures and culture realms, economic activities, and social forms. Human geography includes numerous subspecialties, including economic geography, political geography, social geography, and cultural geography.

HUMAN-ENVIRONMENT RELATIONS

Many geographers address relationships between human activities and the natural environment. Frequently, early geographers attempted to relate observed settlement patterns, cultural practices, religious beliefs, racial distributions, and so forth to the climate, landforms, and resources in which societies were located. For example, the ancient Greeks divided the world into three zonal belts: the torrid, the temperate, and the frigid. These belts were said to explain some of the personality characteristics and cultural variability noted by early explorers.

Geographic determinism survived into the twentieth century in American geography. The writings of the important American geographer Ellen Churchill Semple exemplify this use of the "land" as a basis of societal form: "The polar regions and the subtropical deserts . . . permit man to form only few and intermittent relations with any one spot, restrict economic methods to the lower stages of development, produce only the small, weak, loosely organized horde, which never evolves into a state so long as it remains in that retarding environment."[2] In other words, Semple argued that it is the resource base that permits the development of society, encourages particular governmental types, and ultimately affects the legal structure of society. Similarly, Semple believed that the climate and resource base of the tropics kept civilization in an undeveloped state, while the temperate zone stimulated the development of civilization.

> Where man has remained in the Tropics, with few exceptions he has suffered arrested development. . . . [Civilization develops] only where Nature subjects man to compulsion, forces him to earn his daily bread, and thereby something more than bread. This compulsion is found in less luxurious but more salutary geographic conditions than the Tropics afford, in an environment that exacts a tribute of labor and invention in return for the boon of life, but offers a reward certain and generous enough to insure the accumulation of wealth which marks the beginning of civilization.[3]

While the writings of environmental determinists such as Semple made for interesting reading and stimulating discussion, they failed to provide an adequate basis for understanding human use of the earth. By the 1920s the philosophy of environmental determinism had been rejected by most geographers. Environmental determinism is currently viewed as an interesting turn in the history of the field but is virtually ignored in contemporary scholarship. At present geographers envision the relationships between society and environment as far more complex than those the environmental determinists posited.

Today geographers who focus on the relationship between society and environment ask a variety of significant questions. How do certain economic activities or cultural practices impact on the physical environment (for example, in increasing or reducing air pollution, toxic hazards, and permanent climatic changes such as desertification)? How does societal and economic structure change the face of the earth? How does the organization of the world economy contribute to land use practices at the local level that may do permanent damage to the environment? How do societies and individuals respond to hazards in the environment such as earthquakes, flooding, and environmental pollution? How are resources identified and used or conserved? Such a list of questions is lengthy but only begins to probe this important portion of the field. Human and physical geographers alike study such topics, and this is the area in which the two portions of the discipline are most closely connected.

In summary, most modern geography can be described as organized around one of two central issues: location in space and human-environmental relationships. The first encompasses issues of where the activity is located, why it is there, and the significance of this location decision. The second includes such issues as how society uses the environment, how the environment as used constrains or enables certain types of activities, and how human activities alter the environment. In each of these cases, geographers seek to understand the impacts of societal structures on spatial arrangements and environmental uses. For this reason, the work of geographers is clearly related to the law, since law represents societal directives and constraints shaping environmental uses and location decisions and encourages stability or change in these relationships.

THE RELATIONSHIP BETWEEN GEOGRAPHY AND LAW

Although geography and law have not been closely linked as disciplines, there are many substantive and theoretical conjunctions between the two fields.[4] Scholars from each have worked together productively. Although Blacksell, Watkins, and Economides have spoken of a "separate development" of the two fields within the social sciences,[5] there are many areas in which collaboration between legal and geographical scholars has the potential for being important for the advancement of both fields.

Researchers have investigated the relationships between law and geography for many years. In the mid 1980s, for example, Grossfeld, a lawyer, posited the influence of geography on the law. He argued in general that differences in geography account for different legal rules. For example, he cited the argument of a German government official to the effect that the use of unleaded gasoline should not be compulsory as had been the case in the United States and Japan. The official pointed out that "because the United States occupies most of a continent and Japan is an island, neither country has to worry much about trips of its citizens into neighboring states and the availability of leaded gas there. Thus differences in geography help account for different legal rules."[6] But Grossfeld went even farther:

> Indeed, geography is fate. Fate not only for a country but also for its culture and its law. A paradigmatic example of geographic–climatic influence is the fact that the Islamic colonization in Spain has never passed the boundary line of olive tree cultivation (41° latitude). Beyond that, the geographic environment colors the law and enables or hinders the transfer of legal institutions.[7]

It is almost inconceivable that contemporary geographers would write in such a vein, since they no longer seek simple causal relationships between the physical environment and human activity. As we have seen, geographers quickly rejected environmental determinism in favor of alternative explanations for human variability.

The rejection of environmental determinism in the relationship between geography and law was evident as early as the late 1920s. Writing in 1928, Wigmore negated any relationship between the evolution of legal systems and environmental characteristics. Wigmore produced a map of the world's laws, arguing that "race" was a primary factor in distinguishing legal systems and secondarily that "natural features" affected the development of law — particularly maritime law.[8] Writing during a period of intense rejection of environmental determinism, Wigmore was careful to limit the connection between the development of legal systems and characteristics of the natural environment. He argued that any causal relationship between physical environment and the legal system was "elusive."[9] Thus Wigmore's characterization of these causal relationships is much more attuned to contemporary geographical thought than is Grossfeld's.

In order to understand the basis of collaboration between law and geography, it is important to specify the areas in which they have common interests and where collaboration could enrich both fields. Blacksell, Watkins, and Economides suggest several lines of potential increased contact between human geography and law.[10] They point out that there are several concepts that geography and law share, including territory, sovereignty, jurisdiction — all concerned with legal issues (law) involving human occupance of the earth (geography). Second, the traditional interest of political geographers in boundary delimitation, boundary conflicts, and the process by which territories are defined or redefined conjoins with the interests of lawyers studying the rules, laws, and procedures creating and enforcing such delimitations. Third, there are three potential contributions that traditional human geography can make to the understanding of law: (1) the mapping of "the distribution and characteristics of users and providers of legal services," (2) the analysis of the association of spatial patterns of legal organization with market forces of social needs, and (3) analyses of the efficiency and utility of the distribution of legal services.

It is clear that there are many other subjects that geographers investigate that are related to the law. Blomley suggests that law frequently has spatial effects, and since law is place-bound, it helps elucidate the nature of the local area.[11] Scholars have also noted the tension between traditional legal discourse and geographic inquiry: "Legal discourse is predicated upon principles of abstraction. Law in that sense constitutes a denial of geography. . . . The tension between theory and practice thus provides one intriguing point for geographically informed contributions."[12] Although the geographer's definition of law as specific to place, context, and locality may be seen as "insurrection" with respect to the law as taught in law schools, legislatures, and law offices, there is nonetheless room for productive interaction between the two fields.[13]

This conjunction of interests is no accident. In fact, there is a clear and consistent relationship between the subject matter of geography and the law, for the underlying processes causing the selection of particular locations for human activities and accelerating environmental change are conditioned by legal structures. In dealing with this set of legislation and administrative procedures, geographers are interested primarily in two types of questions. First, what are the spatial or environmental impacts of particular laws and their enforcement patterns? Second, what are the social, political, economic, and cultural conditions that cause laws to be formulated and enforced? Focusing in particular on land use and environmental laws, let us deal with each of these major questions in turn.

THE IMPACTS OF PARTICULAR STATUTES

Geographers routinely study the enactment, enforcement, and impacts of laws dealing with environmental regulations and land use. Many studies focus on the actual impacts of attempts by the federal government to reduce human exposure to natural hazards. Geographers have documented noncompliance or resistance to compliance with legislation, factors involved in the development of legislation, and unintended consequences of legislation in land use or planning practice. A few examples of empirical studies by geographers document the range of interest within academic geography in the development, implementation, and enforcement of such regulations.

The first type of study is the documentation of responses to regulations devised by the Federal Emergency Management Agency (FEMA) and other federal and state agencies in order to reduce flood damage through the encouragement of better land use. Driever and Vaughn described how the Kansas City government permitted residential and commercial real estate development in the floodplain despite repeated, damaging flooding and also how city officials resisted federal efforts to reduce flood hazards. When forced by National Flood Insurance Program (NFIP) regulations to produce flood insurance maps and develop ordinances to regulate development in the floodplains, officials were unresponsive: "Unwilling to modify existent floodplain development, especially at its own expense, the city placated FEMA with a modes program that focused on the use of building permits to limit new construction on the lower floodplain. The permit system was so flagrantly administered that some new construction violated NFIP guidelines."[14] Thus Driever and Vaughn concluded that despite attempts by the federal government to provide a form of insurance and demand the local specification of an associated land use management policy, local jurisdictions have taken every possible measure to avoid the impact of the law.

A second type of study considers both the ways in which the legislation was developed and passed and also the general structure of the political economy and the forces that shape response to particular legislation within an advanced capitalist economy. Platt has documented the development of flood regulations and the role of a key individual on executive and legislative processes.[15] He outlined the changing nature of federal legislation regulating flood policy and discussed the influential role of geographer Gilbert F. White. Platt described the significant policy shift from engineering solutions such as dams, reservoirs, levees, and channelization to *nonstructural measures* such as insurance, land use regulation, and disaster assistance programs. He attributed much of this shift from structural to nonstructural adjustments to White, who was involved academically and professionally in positions where research and policy could be brought together and could thereby have a major influence on emerging policy.[16]

A third type of study investigates the unintended and yet predictable results of legislation, which vary depending on the extent to which the legislation is discordant with the general processes of the political economy. Legislation that reinforces existing processes is most effective; legislation that runs counter to the smooth functioning of the political economy and the interests of major economic stakeholders is likely to be ineffective. Individuals and corporations continue to pursue their economic interests despite legislation that may divert them from their intended goals; when one avenue is blocked, they simply find another.

An example of this type of study is the documentation of the impacts of federal law attempting to reduce susceptibility to natural hazards. The Coastal Barrier Resources Act of 1981 attempted to impose restrictions on the development of land susceptible to coastal flooding.[17] The act was intended to supplement the Omnibus Budget Reconciliation Act of 1981[18] by identifying undeveloped coastal barriers where federal flood insurance and federal development subsidies would not be available for new construction or substantial improvements to existing dwellings.

Coastal barriers are islands or landforms that are connected to the mainland bordering the Atlantic and Gulf coasts from Maine to Texas. Examples of such areas include the popular resorts of Hilton Head, South Carolina; Marco Island and Amelia Island, Florida; as well as areas such as Atlantic City, New Jersey; Galveston, Texas; and Scituate, Massachusetts. Since these areas are particularly susceptible to coastal flooding associated with hurricanes, they may be especially dangerous for permanent or even seasonal occupance.

The Coastal Barrier Resources Act was intended to halt or at least slow construction in these highly dangerous areas. Yet Platt pointed out:

> Exposure of lives and investments to risk from natural hazards is increasing on most developed coastal barriers due to infilling of vacant land, intensification of already developed land, and rising property values of existing development. The federal government is continuing to contribute indirectly to this situation by providing the various benefits in developed areas that are now prohibited on undeveloped barriers. Furthermore, denial of such benefits in the CBRS [Coastal Barrier Resources System — the shoreline identified by the act as "undeveloped"] actually reinforces pressures for further development on developed coastal barriers.[19]

Thus legislation that was supposed to reduce the exposure of human life and property to destruction associated with hurricanes has had just the opposite effect: It has concentrated property development and population in the already developed areas, increasing the risk of loss of life and property. When it is impossible to develop "undeveloped barriers," the natural response is to intensify development on "developed barriers," with the consequence of increased land values and demand for areas that are equally unsafe.

A second example of studies of unintended impacts of legislation or the failure of legislation to achieve the desired end is the documentation of the impacts of California state legislation intended to reduce earthquake hazards. The Alquist-Priolo Special Studies Zones Act, passed in 1972 and modified in 1975, required that surface fault rupture zones be identified and mapped and that real estate agents disclose the locations of these zones to prospective buyers. The purpose of the act was to set up a program of mapping surface traces of active faults and to halt further construction of large-scale public facilities or large-scale residential projects astride the identified fault traces. It was also meant to inform prospective buyers of the location of these zones, presumably to increase awareness of earthquake hazards.

While the legislation has succeeded in the sense that a mapping program was established and construction directly astride surface fault traces has presumably been halted, the broader purposes of the legislation have not been fulfilled. The disclosure provisions were intended to inform prospective buyers that the existing structures they were purchasing were within the zones — that is, that there were hazards associated with the area. Yet survey research has demonstrated that developers have made few if any modifications in their plans as a result of the locations of the zones.[20] In fact, according to state and county officials, they have put lifelines such as highways and pipelines along fault traces, transferring risk from the private homeowner to the public at large.[21]

Furthermore, location in the zones does not affect home mortgage decisions or rates, appraisals, prices, or buyer demand.[22] Home buyers frequently do not remember the disclosure, and it has virtually no impact on decisions to buy insurance or take other mitigation measures.[23] Real estate agents state that they favor the mandatory disclosures because this requirement does not adversely affect business and, furthermore, the signed disclosure form may protect them from subsequent liability if the house is destroyed or damaged in a major earthquake. The legislation, while well-meaning, has been neutralized within the real estate process, where the overwhelming influence of the political economy reduces the impact of any legislation that might interfere with its smooth functioning. This research is another example of the interest in having geographers examine the background of legislation and its impact on the interaction between environment and society.

Geographers have also studied legislation affecting land use and development. Such legislation might include growth control regulations, variability in property taxation, or other development restrictions that affect the distribution of activities.

The geographic literature on the impacts of particular taxation and land use regulations is vast, documenting both the successes and failures of such legislation to achieve its stated aims.[24] One example of this literature is the study of the attempt to use taxation to improve mass transit in Los Angeles. Adler analyzed the history of local and state legislation related to the establishment of rapid transit, noting the critical opposition of business and property groups outside the central business district.[25] Even when the Los Angeles Metropolitan Transit Authority was finally established in 1951, it was constrained in power and financing authority.

When the state responded to growing needs by establishing the Southern California Rapid Transit District in 1964, it nonetheless limited the influence of representation from the Los Angeles central business district by placing only two representatives from the city of Los Angeles on an eleven-member board. Perhaps not surprisingly, the district was granted neither sales nor property-taxing power to subsidize its operations. The most recent successor, the Los Angeles County Transportation Commission, was created by the state legislature in 1976. The commission was granted more power in its authorization to impose a sales tax in order to subsidize service. Its power has been eroded, however, in the regional tax-base sharing plan and the attempts by the city to remove express bus service operations from the district and into its own jurisdiction.

Without going into further detail on this case, we can see that it represents an intense struggle between downtown and suburban commercial interests, with side issues of serving a transit-dependent population, the enticement of federal subsidies, as well as environmental protection — all combined in the transmutation of legislation into actual practice. Adler concluded that we need to look at the way legislation is passed and how it is implemented but that it is also necessary to analyze the reasons for its successes and failures by reference to geographic processes such as spatial competition and the operation of societal processes. Our understanding of the law is thus enriched by a geographic analysis of its consequences.

A second example of geographic analysis of a set of land use regulations is a study of the impacts of growth control legislation in California. Exline studied the evolution of the growth limitation plan of Petaluma, California, concluding that the environmentally motivated legislation resulted in a rapid escalation of house prices with a concomitant exclusion of lower-income families from the area.[26] Because of the complex interactions and implications of the legislation, unusual coalitions of proponents and opponents were formed, with environmentalists and developers allied at times. Many other studies of the impacts of zoning and growth limitation have been completed by geographers, most concluding that the environmental and social goals of the legislation were incompatible.

Another important contribution of geographic analysis to evaluating land use regulations is in the study of the interaction between water law and urbanization in the American West. Wescoat has described the complex and evolving relationships between water law and urban development, concluding that conflicting pressures exist. Tension between efforts to restrict the transfer of water over long distances and efforts to relax constraints on the place of water use has created a collision among urban, environmental, and rural interests in a variety of geographic contexts.[27]

THE EVOLUTION OF LAWS IN SOCIETY

These examples have shown that many geographers have an interest in the origin and effects of legislation regulating land use or intended to conserve resources or reduce human susceptibility to environmental hazards. A second and more fundamental interest of geographers is in the ways laws are developed in society and their significance as a reflection of power and the functioning of various interest groups.

Why particular laws are enacted and how they are enforced are even more significant to geography than the more straightforward analysis of the impacts of laws on societal, spatial, or environmental structure, although less work has been done on this topic. This question is of interest to philosophers, students of jurisprudence, and sociologists, for the answers to it reflect the nature of law in society — the ways in which laws demonstrate societal values, the impacts of minority or majority opinion on law, issues of power relationships, as well as the most general concerns of societal structure and organization.

The question is also of interest to geographers who see spatial structures and environmental practices as integral to the processes by which individuals and structures interact. Laws represent an attempt by those empowered to govern (whether through civil authority given to the government by a willing populace, civil authority imposed through a variety of economic and military controls, or religious authority imposed or accepted) to codify standards of behavior, duty, exchange, and privilege. The existence of a given law is a signal that at a particular time an issue generated debate and disagreement that was resolved through legislation. Of course the evolution of law — whether through changes in the code itself, modifications in interpretation made by courts, or changes in enforcement — also represents shifts in the nature of society and the relationships between individuals and between individuals and their environment. In this sense, all of the law is of interest to geographers who need to understand the full range of societal constraints and enablements in order to pursue more limited questions.

Geographers' interest in the law as one of several indicators of societal structure is related to the philosophical perspective of realism, which rejects the simple study of objects and their associations in space and time, instead probing the nature of the structure through what can be observed. As Gregory has argued, "Realism insists that properly scientific explanations can (and must) disclose causal mechanisms and structures that, typically, are beyond observation."[28] Thus although we can find a spatial association between a particular legal structure (e.g., inheritance taxes) and land use practices (the divestiture of property by the elderly to avoid such taxes), the more significant questions we must ask to explain land use practices are why and how such legal structures evolved as they did, how they reflect power structures within society, and then how these values and structures are translated into law, its enforcement, and individual response.

Literature in this portion of geography tends to describe the nature of society, the structure of the capitalist political economy, the forces that shape urban development, and the role of various interest and power groups in affecting the structures that constrain and enable individual behavior. For example, in his classic work on the implications of Marxian theory for human geography, David Harvey describes the legal system as providing the support of capitalist relations:

> "Juridical individuals" (persons, corporations, etc.) must be able to approach each other on an equal footing in exchange, as sole and exclusive owners of commodities with the freedom to buy from and sell to whomsoever they please. For such a condition to exist supposes not only a solid legal foundation to exchange but also the power to sustain private property rights and enforce contracts. This power, of course, resides in "the state." [29]

In short, the legal and political structure provides a buttress that permits the political economy to function and the marketplace to exist.

Harvey also describes the impacts of the legal system in the process of expansion and accumulation:

> The political history of colonialism and imperialism provides an interesting illustration of the problem. Military conquest establishes state control. Surveyors establish private property in land (the laborer can then be excluded from the land by rent), transport and communication links are built, legal systems (conducive to exchange, of course) are established, and precapitalist populations proletarianized and disciplined (by force and repression, if necessary, but also through law, education, missionary activity, and the like). All of this costs vast sums of money. Beneath its surface ideological justifications, therefore, the politics of capitalist imperialism amount to a vast, long-run speculative investment which may or may not pay off. [30]

Here the legal system is seen as supporting capitalist expansion, promoting the restructuring of spatial organization.

Another quite different perspective on the role of the legal system in the overall societal structure is Clark's analysis of two rulings concerning local autonomy in Chicago and Toronto. [31] The Chicago case involved a fight by one of the suburbs against the siting of a water treatment plant by the sewerage authority. The Toronto case involved a dispute over the size of a shopping center to be located in a suburban area. Although both involved similar kinds of jurisdictional disputes in similar political economic settings, the results of the cases were quite different. In the Toronto case, the presiding judge ruled that the higher governmental power could not require certain planning activities, upholding the city's claim. In the Chicago case, after many hearings and appeals, the Supreme Court found in favor of the district rather than the city, denying the city's claims to regulate local land use. Despite structural similarities in the cases, then, different judgments were made concerning the proper level of jurisdiction.

Clark concluded that these differences result from a series of principles. First is "judicial incapacity." Rulings are not unambiguous, and there are often debates about the applicability of rules to different situations. Second, there is an "incoherence of principles" — contradictions built into a set of rules may sometimes make decisions seem to be arbitrary and capricious. Third, there is "analytical abstraction," the separation between the principles that are generally used to guide action and the application of rules to particular situations. Clark thus concludes that "just knowing the political structure of different cities or different countries is not enough to derive their likely similarities and differences."[32]

Related to this general notion of law as an indicator of societal structure is the study of the spatial variability in implementation of particular laws. As we have already noted, geography deals with the character of individual places at particular times. Geography describes the local context, a context important in understanding the enforcement of the law. Blomley has outlined the nature of local factors in the variability of legal interpretation — that is, the translation of the law from an abstraction to applicability to a particular case. Since the court not only attempts to interpret the text of the law but also its substantive meaning, there is room for interpretation reflecting the context of the local society. In the case of the Shops Act in England (which involves closing businesses on Sunday), Blomley argues that the judges had to ask themselves how the law applied to the interests of the local inhabitants, invoking a "contextual nature of statutory interpretation." He admonishes geographers to avoid interpretation of law as if there were no spatial variations in its implementation and effect; instead, "the application and interpretation of law can be seen to have a distinct spatial and contextual nature."[33]

Even more generally, Johnston has analyzed a set of court decisions related to residential segregation.[34] He explains a series of Supreme Court decisions that have failed to interfere with the autonomy of suburban districts (thereby preserving de facto racial segregation in housing and schools) as reflecting the political balance and ideology of society. Johnston concludes that social organizations such as the courts attempt to maintain the status quo in order to preserve the power of the already powerful. The courts have bolstered this conservative trend, partly because the justices and judges themselves operate within the constraints of societal values. As Johnston summarizes it:

Overall it is clear that the decisions taken have favoured the status quo. [This is because] the ideology which [the Supreme Court justices and judges of the various other courts] operate, into which they have been socialized, and which they demonstrated to their patrons/ constituents, strongly favours the status quo. The justices have been put there, and the texts that they have to interpret have been written, to provide stability, to mediate conflicts in such a way that the strength of the system is enhanced.[35]

Thus the workings of the court and the interpretations of statutes are seen from the perspective of the societal whole — the workings of a particular institutional structure or political and economic organization in a particular place. This kind of interpretation of a set of court cases provides a fascinating and important window through which to interpret both the operation of this society as well as its spatial and environmental organization.

CONCLUSION

Although there has been relatively little interaction between the formal disciplines of geography and law, both fields have strong overlapping interests. We have noted that geography may be defined as a discipline with two primary missions: the study of the spatial distribution of phenomena and the analysis of the relationships between society and the environment. Geographers have focused on several significant research questions related to the study of law, including the spatial implications of legislation and court decisions, particularly land use and environmental regulations, as well as the ways in which the operation of the legal system reflects and is shaped by the general nature of society.

Human geography has involved both the search for spatial regularities and general principles as well as an understanding of the interplay of place or local area with general structure. Some have argued that the recent emphasis in human geography on place and locale may conflict with the vision of law as a search for general principles rather than locally derived insights. However, it is clear that both fields are increasingly informed by critical social theory, a development that promises the possibility of more fertile intellectual discourse.

Geography can contribute to and benefit from legal research not only in the more traditional areas of overlap — that is, in the analysis of the impacts of particular pieces of legislation or court decisions — but also, increasingly, in the interactions among law, legal discourse, and the nature of place or locale. Each field has important insights to offer the other, and both will be enriched by even closer interaction.

NOTES

1.   Richard Hartshorne (1959), Perspective on the Nature of Geography. Chicago: Rand McNally.

2.   Ellen Churchill Semple (1911), Influences of Geographic Environment: On the Basis of Ratzel's System of Anthropogeography. New York: Henry Holt and Company.

3.   Ibid.

4.   Nicholas K. Blomley (1993), "Making Space for Law," Urban Geography, 14, pp. 3–6.

5.   Mark Blacksell, Charles Watkins, and Kim Economides (1986), "Human Geography and Law: A Case of Separate Development in Social Science," Progress in Human Geography, 10, pp. 373–396.

6.   Bernhard Grossfeld (1984), "Geography and Law," Michigan Law Review, 82, pp. 1510–1519.

7.   Grossfeld (1984), op. cit.

8.   John Henry Wigmore (1928), A Panorama of the World's Legal Systems (Washington, D.C.: Washington Law Book Company); John Henry Wigmore (1929), "A Map of the World's Law," Geographical Review, 19, pp. 114–120.

9.   Wigmore (1929).

10. Blacksell, Watkins, and Economides (1986).

11. Blomley (1993).

12. Nicholas K. Blomley and Gordon L. Clark (1990), "Law, Theory and Geography," Urban Geography, 11, pp. 433–446.

13. W. Wesley Pue (1990), "Wrestling with Law, Geographical. Specificity vs. Legal. Abstraction," Urban Geography, 11, pp. 566–585.

14. Steven L. Driever and Danny M. Vaughn (1988), "Flood Hazard in Kansas City Since 1860," Geographical Review, 78, pp. 1–19.

15. Rutherford H. Platt (1986), "Floods and Man: A Geographer's Agenda," in Geography, Resources and Environment, edited by Robert H. Kates and Ian Burton. Chicago: University of Chicago Press, pp. 28–68.

16. Ibid.

17. Coastal Barrier Resources Act of 1981, 16 U.S.C. §§3501–3510 (1981).

18. Omnibus Budget Reconciliation Act of 1981, 42 U.S.C. §4028 (1981).

19. Rutherford H. Platt (1987), "Overview," in Cities on the Beach: Management Issues of Developed Coastal Barriers, edited by Rutherford H. Platt, Sheila G. Pelczarski, and Barbara K.R. Burbank. Chicago: University of Chicago, Department of Geography, Research Paper 224, pp. 1–14.

20. Risa Palm (1988), "Alquist Priolo Legislation on Active Fault Zones," Proceedings, National Earthquake Hazards Reduction Program: 1977–87, United States Geological Survey, Open File 88-13-A, pp. 225–230.

21. Ibid.

22. Risa Palm et al. (1983), "The Response of Lenders and Appraisers to Earthquake Hazards," University of Colorado, Institute of Behavioral Science, Monograph 38.

23. Risa Palm (1982), "Real Estate Agents and Special Studies Zones," University of Colorado, Institute of Behavioral Science, Monograph 32.

24. Some of this work is cited or summarized in Robert Lake (ed.) (1993), Resolving Locational Conflict (New Brunswick: Rutgers University Center for Urban Policy Research); Rutherford H. Platt (1991), Land Use Control: Geography, Law and Public Policy (Englewood Cliffs, New Jersey: Prentice Hall); and John B. Wright (1993), Rocky Mountain Divide: Selling and Saving the West (Austin: University of Texas Press).

25. S. Adler (1986), "The Dynamics of Transit Innovation in Los Angeles," Society and Space, 4, pp. 321–335.

26. Christopher Exline (1978), "The Impacts of Growth Control Legislation on Two Suburban Communities," Ph.D. dissertation, Department of Geography, University of California–Berkeley.

27. James L. Wescoat Jr. (1993), "Water Law, Urbanization and Urbanism in the American West: The 'Place of Use' Revisited," Urban Geography, 14, pp. 414–420.

28. Derek Gregory (1983), "Realism," in Dictionary of Human Geography, edited by R. J. Johnston, Derek Gregory, and David M. Smith. Oxford: Basil Blackwell.

29. David Harvey (1982), The Limits to Capital. Chicago: University of Chicago Press.

30. Ibid.

31. Gordon L. Clark (1986), "Adjudicating Jurisdictional Disputes in Chicago and Toronto: Legal Formalism and Urban Structure," Urban Geography, 7, pp. 63–80.

32. Ibid.

33. Nicholas K. Blomley (1987), "Legal Interpretation: The Geography of Law," Tijdschrift voor Economische en Sociale Geografie, 78.

34. R. J. Johnston (1984), Residential Segregation, the State and Constitutional Conflict in American Urban Areas. London: Academic Press.

35. Ibid.

2

WHAT IS LAW? PRELIMINARY THOUGHTS ON GEOJURISPRUDENTIAL PERSPECTIVES

W. WESLEY PUE

The character of law seems obvious to most everyone at a commonsense level. Yet the precise connotations of that term or of "legal studies" are elusive. Meaning constantly slips out of reach when jurist, citizen, or social theorist attempts to define the terms or to justify what they are doing when engaged in research of the "legal" — or, more difficult still — "sociolegal" sorts.

While poets may perhaps be forgiven a considerable degree of muddleheadedness in approaching such an arcane inquiry, it will be disturbing to nonspecialists to learn that anything even remotely approaching a definition of "law" has eluded the leading social scientists and jurists of the century. H.L.A. Hart, for example, arguably the twentieth century's leading jurisprudential thinker in the English language, evaded the task of providing a definition in his seminal book *The Concept of Law.* With regard to the question, "What is law?" he asserted simply that "nothing concise enough to be recognized as a definition could provide a satisfactory answer," for "the underlying issues are too different from each other and too fundamental to be capable of this sort of resolution."[1] Similarly, Roger Cotterell, a leading modern sociologist of law, explicitly denies both the possibility and the utility of seeking a definition of "law." Instead, Cotterell opts to work only on the basis of "working models" that facilitate and organize inquiry but may be abandoned willy-nilly when their utility for concrete purposes seems in doubt.[2]

Recognizing that there is a degree of truth in the old adage "Fools rush in where angels fear to tread," I, too, will decline the temptation to offer any all-embracing definition of "law." Rather, what I offer here are preliminary thoughts on perspectives about law that may be particularly fruitful in directing

---

This chapter is adapted with permission from W. Wesley Pue, "Towards Geo-Jurisprudence? Formalizing Research Agendas in Law and Geography," *Windsor Review of Legal and Social Issues/ Revue des affaires juridiques et sociales — Windsor* 3 (1991): 71-93.

work in the dynamic interdisciplinary field of law and geography. The avenues that I believe deserve special attention from pioneers in this new subdiscipline have recently been thrown into prominence in the larger field of law and society, and I accordingly offer a brief — albeit idiosyncratic — account of the recent history of thought about the character of law, indicating some sources of conceptual confusion and practical modern responses to it. I then highlight some specific implications of this work for geographical research agendas.

REVIEW OF ATTEMPTS TO DEFINE LAW

Until relatively recent times, narrow disciplinary expertise was valued less than wide-ranging intellectual acquisition. The precise delineation of disciplinary boundaries seemed not to be a matter of great concern to the literate classes in the Anglo-American world. Eloquent testimony to this is found in an 1846 report of the English Committee on Legal Education, which endorsed the view of Sir George Stephen that "the [legal] Profession should be so educated as to be qualified for carrying on . . . intercourse as gentlemen themselves; but I apprehend that qualification cannot be attained except by educating them as gentlemen, with much greater attention to their general endowments and information than is at present the case."[3] The same report put forward the committee's own view that university professors of law should be expected to demonstrate expertise in history, philosophy, "Political Geography, Statistics and Political Economy"![4] In early days it seemed unremarkable that lawyers were significant players in the development of the disciplines we now think of as the social sciences.[5]

For reasons that need not detain us here, it became increasingly important to common-lawyers during the Victorian era to define more precisely where their expertise lay and to develop more rigid borders of demarcation between law and nonlaw.[6] In both of the leading common-law countries (the United States and England) as well as in those parts of the world touched by their imperialist reaches, the definition of "law" as operationalized by lawyers, law professors, and jurists became significantly narrowed and increasingly distanced from the related disciplines of political science, sociology, economics, history, philosophy, and geography.[7]

The apogee of this lawyers' intellectual apartheid was perhaps most clearly articulated by Christopher Columbus Langdell's characterization of law as a science that draws upon the "empirical" data of the reports of cases decided by appellate courts to find the "right" answers to legal problems. This extreme manifestation of positivism defined the lawyers' task as one of identifying the content of common law and radically excised this descriptive task from principles of legislation, politics, moral philosophy, and such like. The legal scholar was to do no more than interpret and provide value-neutral, objective, logical classifications of legal principles.[8] The juridicopolitical corollary of this was the denial that judges rendering decisions were engaged in activities that involved elements of choice and the assertion that the art of judicial decisionmaking was more or less scientific, objective, and subject to evaluation for "correctness." Courts were conceived of as machines in which the factual backgrounds of particular disputes were mixed with law to produce neatly packaged, appropriate, noncontroversial, apolitical, dehumanized, and correct decisions. Among university law teachers, legal practitioners, and judges, this came to be the dominant paradigm, notwithstanding numerous rearguard actions that were fought more or less constantly from the beginning.

Such a stultified approach was not, of course, acceptable to thoughtful observers of law in human societies. In other disciplines concerned with the role of law in society (such as sociology and anthropology) the legalistic myopia that amputated law from cognate social sciences was never a serious contender for scholarly respectability. Even in the heart of the legal academy, significant challenges were raised to the limited conceptualization of "law" associated with the Langdell case method. Prominent judges and scholars such as Oliver Wendell Holmes and Roscoe Pound found the notion that judges could arrive at "right" decisions in cases before them to be quite indefensible and rejected the mechanical notion of judicial decisionmaking as fanciful. Holmes, for example, in an extraordinary article asserted simply that "the prophecies of what the courts will do in fact, and nothing more pretentious, are what I mean by law."[9] During the first three or four decades of the twentieth century, the sociological jurisprudence associated with Pound and his disciples was succeeded by an aggressive and effective attack on "Langdellian" classical conceptions of law by "American legal realists" who rejected outright the position that judicial decisionmaking stood somehow above personal preference and policy bias and who actively sought out ways to influence public policy through law. "Realism" poured out everywhere. An experiment in developing a scholarly empirical social science of law was launched and lapsed at Yale, and a generation of law faculty moved into New Deal public service. With their success in shaping public policy, however, their jurisprudential flood subsided.[10]

Outside of the legal profession and law schools, other scholars continued to address issues that related to law. They usually took approaches which were considerably more open-ended, less obsessed with the processes of applying and classifying caselaw than was the norm among lawyers.[11] While nonlawyers only occasionally made "law" the focal point of their studies, their attempts to conceptualize law and legality are instructive.[12] Even a cursory review of nonlegal literature reveals that the social sciences bring significantly different understandings of the nature of law to bear in defining the objects of their study. Generally speaking, the lawyer's obsession with judges, courts, and caselaw is reduced in social science literature and replaced with a correspondingly greater emphasis on the state, legislatures, and bureaucrats or, more generally, with rules, norms, or understandings that actually affect people's behavior.

The leading figure in American functionalist sociology, Talcott Parsons, offered a definition of "law" as "a set of rules backed by certain types of sanctions, legitimized in certain ways and applied in certain ways." Emphasizing the notion that law involves a general application of "patterns, norms and rules" to "all sectors of society," Parsons continued to indicate that he thought laws must emanate from "duly authorized" legislative bodies and must be put into effect by bodies that interpret rules and determine their applicability to individuals.[13] This approach has obvious strengths in comparison to the classical legal paradigm in its emphasis on rule formulation (and hence policy choice) and in allowing for the consideration of rule interpretation and application by state officials and others apart from the appellate courts. However, it, too, ultimately perpetuates a narrow vision of law and legality. Parsons's sociology of law proceeds within a perspective that limits the operation of law to "social control" functions. There is limited room here for a vision of law as facilitative of private ordering, as "institutionalized ideology," as arena of struggle, or as cultural artifact. Moreover, it may be that the Parsons approach is more state-centered than it ought to be.

In these respects, the perspective of Selznick that law exists "in the structure of many different groups and associations" and that it is not simply a feature of "the political structure of the state" moves considerably further away from the lawyers' paradigm than does Parsons's approach. This is even more apparent in light of Selznick's further assertion that law "is oriented more toward the persuasive than toward the coercive end of the social control continuum."[14] To similar effect, though more explicitly, Ehrlich has argued that law exists in many institutions that seem at first sight at least to be at some distance removed from the state. For him, law consists of "the rules, etc., which actually order or regulate a society; in particular the rules which constitute the inner ordering of associations (i.e., corporations, churches, family, etc.) that regulate society. . . . The inner order of associations represents true law (i.e., 'living law') as opposed to lawyer's law. . . . This would give the appearance that any social control of a group, association, or institution constitutes law."[15]

MODERN APPROACHES TO LEGAL STUDIES

There is a sort of inevitable logic by which these perspectives on the nature of law are drawn ever further from the mainstream legal tradition's positivist emphasis on sovereign commands[16] and the adjudicative behavior of judges. When social scientists rather than lawyers (whose working lives are court-centered) look at the legal system, they are likely to be concerned with issues relating to the origins of law on the one hand and the concrete effects of legal rules — on individuals, classes, ethnic groups, economic actors, environment, or human "space" — on the other. From here it is but a short step to the realization that the actual regulation of human society is affected by forces and persons outside the formal "legal order," and hence (to use Ehrlich's approach) "true law" is both multifaceted and derived from many sources.[17]

More recently, however, a series of approaches derived from various developments in the area of state theory have begun to question the degree to which conceptualizations of law should be limited to emphasis on regulation, social control, or — generally — the exercise of authority in a top-down sort of relationship. Important contributions by social historians and, more recently, "critical legal theorists" have drawn attention to the importance of law not just as rules, orders, sanctions, and threats but as an intellectual or ideological force that impacts significantly upon and interacts diffusely with other spheres of intellectual and ideological endeavor.[18] As theories of ideology have become more sophisticated and increasingly distanced from simplistic notions of "mystification" or "false consciousness,"[19] law has come to be more frequently described through metaphors emphasizing dynamic interaction, "arenas of struggle," and cultural engagement.[20] As Phil Harris writes, modern theorists of law in society are more likely to be concerned with the processes by which social consensus is developed and shaped than with the old questions as to whether any given society is "fundamentally" characterized by consensus or conflict of values.[21]

A related and crucially important element added to the mix of ingredients that now give flavor to debates about the nature of law is a strong and persuasive "critical" rejection of one particular lawyer's categorization of long-standing central importance: the so-called public-private distinction.[22] Two consequences flow from this. First, scholarly attention is clearly directed toward a consideration of the public consequences of legal arrangements in the so-called private-law area.[23] Second, and closely related, a rejection of the public-private distinction has the consequence of reinforcing the assault on the "legal-nonlegal" categorization that characterizes the work of theorists such as Selznick and Ehrlich.[24] Both of these tendencies have been reinforced by "postmodern" theorizing, with its emphasis on the "microphysics" of power, frequently exercised in the interstices of law and social organization.[25]

Corresponding to this, legal theorists have come to emphasize not just public policy writ large but the public policy impacts of accumulation of small-scale human interactions (often themselves conditioned in part by the legal environment). Such research has served to draw attention not just to the important public implications of "private-law" doctrine (in areas such as property law, trusts, contract law, the law of torts, and family law) but also to the importance of recognizing a pervasive legal pluralism wherein "law" is recognized at many levels both within and without the state.[26]

FUTURE RESEARCH AGENDAS IN LAW AND GEOGRAPHY

These new developments in theorizing in and about law have important implications for research agendas in the field of law and geography. While one effect is to make the task of geojurisprudence more difficult, it seems that the engagement of geographical researchers with social and legal theory about the nature, role, and functions of law and state promises to provide a much firmer foundation for geojurisprudential research than would otherwise be the case.

Recognition of the sorts of concerns emphasized by modern theoretical formulations leads to practical as well as theoretical linkages between the two disciplines and creates the possibility for cross-disciplinary research and intellectual engagement that will make fundamental and crucially important contributions to both disciplines in their many subfields. A sophisticated approach to legal theory opens the door to vast new spaces of potential geographical research just as an appreciation on the part of lawyers for geography as a core social science (not just as being "about maps") suggests whole new vistas of jurisprudential understanding. Engagement at these levels holds forth the promise that geographers can contribute not just technical knowledge and "expert" input in discrete applied areas of policy formulation, but that they can also play a role in defining the very nature of research agendas in the wider field of law and society. Geography and law will both benefit by critical and theoretical engagement as disciplines of coequal status in which neither is "on top" nor "on tap."[27]

The field will, however, be stifled from the beginning if narrow and legalistic approaches to law are allowed to hold sway. It is to the credit of geographers who have begun to look at law as part of their research that many have attempted to grapple seriously with literature originating among legal scholars. But in doing so there is a danger of falling captive to work that is given most prominence among lawyers still overly influenced by the anti-intellectualism of the legal tradition rather than taking on board legal research that engages more openly and more broadly with the larger world of scholarly inquiry.

In this respect, it is particularly important for geographers to escape the lawyer's obsession with what judges do. Important literature though this is, a myopic focus on the dynamics of judicial decisionmaking,[28] on the desirable relationship between law and morality, or on the intrinsic nature of rules provides too narrow a basis for interdisciplinary engagement. Stultifying debate that concentrates exclusively on scholars such as Bentham, Mill, Hart, Fuller, Devlin, Dworkin, or Posner has, I think, been overemphasized in the nascent law and geography literature. While there is certainly truth, for example, in Dworkin's assertion that "law is an interpretive concept," scholars who are not trapped within the intellectual box[29] of the professional law school will wish to look considerably beyond the narrow starting point on which this sort of theory is developed. Dworkin — like most lawyers who approach the question, "What is law?" — begs the question by constraining his discussion to court-centered issues and inquiries. Dworkin, at any rate, has the merit of being explicit: "Judges should decide what the law is by interpreting the practice of other judges deciding what the law is. General theories of law, for us, are general interpretations of our own judicial practice."[30] Though Dworkin's work is much cited in the new literature on law and geography,[31] any definition of law derived from such a limited starting point clearly restricts inquiry in ways that more open-ended approaches do not.

This is not, however, to assert that issues of interpretation are irrelevant to the study of law or of law and geography, only that the framework of an interpreta-tion-based approach to law and legality should reach considerably beyond nar-row issues of judicial — or legislative — practice. In concluding this chapter, I wish to argue for further work in three areas of law and geography. First, it seems important that work in the nature of impact analyses should continue and be expanded. Second, I argue that there is a need for a developed geopolitical economy of law grounded in concrete historical study. Third, at least some "geojurisprudential" researchers should reach beyond limited conceptualiza-tions of law to embrace an open-ended legal pluralism as their starting point when they conceive and define research projects.

IMPACT ANALYSIS

Perhaps the best-established area of research at the law-geography interface lies in the field of impact analysis, wherein the actual effect of legislation on the ground is evaluated by geographers and compared with the intent of legislators. Geographers seek out discrepancies and either suggest new legal approaches to known problems or identify previously unrecognized problem areas where legal intervention seems socially or environmentally warranted. The bulk of the present volume provides a powerful demonstration of the value and variety of research that can be conducted within the "impact analysis" framework. In Chapter 1 Risa Palm has given eloquent and succinct expression to the episte-mological rationale of this approach in arguing that "the work of geographers is clearly related to the law" because "law represents societal directives and con-straints shaping environmental uses and location decisions and encourages stabil-ity or change in these relationships."[32]

Studies of this sort have inestimable concrete value, and while some have argued that geojurisprudential research should go beyond impact analysis,[33] there is little doubt either that geographers bring to such work skills not found in any other discipline or that such research can produce clear, tangible results for the "environmental" experiences of large numbers of people. The contributions to this volume provide persuasive testimony of the potential for this kind of work to enhance understanding in such crucial areas of social life as law of the sea, international protection of human rights, interstate boundary demarcation, crime, planning, environmental protection, resource exploitation, agriculture, and the provision of legal services.[34]

With regard to impact studies, however, I think it might be valuable for geographers consciously to attempt to apply their techniques and expertise in "legal" fields with which they are less familiar. At a minimum, geographers should stretch their conceptions of law by attempting to incorporate common-law and especially "private-law" doctrines in geographical analysis. This is a tall order and may perhaps be especially difficult for individuals without any formal legal training, but the potential is so great that the area seems to merit some form of incorporation into the corpus of geographical work about law.

The need for such inquiries has not been entirely unrecognized by geographers whose work touches on law. Thus, for example, Clark and Dear have called upon researchers to go beyond Teitz's[35] conception of law involving state as spatial regulator, and for very good reason: "But of course the impact of law does not only relate to those laws promulgated to regulate and control social and economic relationships directly. The whole legal system affects individual behavior and the arrangements of relationships and interdependence between individuals and classes."[36]

In truth, however, this insight is more frequently noted than its challenge taken up, and variations in local impact — as well as the general spatial implications — of private-law doctrines (affecting, for example, the law of contract or of wills and intestate succession) remain to be pursued. While it is relatively easy, following in the footsteps of certain legal historians, to assert relationships of one sort or another between "law" and "capitalism,"[38] specifically geographical dimensions of such research have never been fully teased out.

(GEO)POLITICAL ECONOMY

As the previous paragraph suggests, at some point specific impact analyses shade into questions at a higher level of generality relating to the relationships among law, economics, politics, and geography, resulting in a need for works that arise from links at the conceptual as well as the applied level of research in both disciplines. At their fringes both law and geography, in common with other social sciences, have been affected by sophisticated theoretical debates relating to questions of historical processes, theory of state, ideology, class, race, gender[37] and discourse.[39]

Theoretical advances of significance throughout the social sciences might be made possible by grounded theorizations that take seriously work in both disciplines. For example, work that explores the linkages among law, geography, and state theory[40] or seeks totally new reformulations of core notions such as that of "city"[41] or perhaps "sovereignty"[42] seems to hold great promise. Some research on women in the workplace[43] has similar potential for introducing reformulations of models in both disciplines, as does work on land tenure systems.[44]

The application of geographical diffusion study techniques might prove valuable in attempting to pin down the nebulous notion of legal ideology both at present and in times past. Geographers are perhaps better equipped than any other group of scholars to seek out the relationships among legal doctrine, legal institutions, the availability of legal services, class, race, gender, space, cultural environment, and commonsense notions of legality and appropriate behavior.[45] This need not be perceived solely as an exercise "mapping" a one-way diffusion of "legal" ideas outward from legal institutions. To engage in such work does not require any particular identification of dependent and independent variables but could conceivably incorporate a dynamic notion of ideology as being constantly in flux and in the process of being negotiated between and among communities that occupy a variety of structural and spatial locations. More broadly still, the location and peculiar characteristics of various discourses about law and social ordering might be explored.

EMBRACING LEGAL PLURALISM

The recognition that legal ideologies and the conditions of the employment of law as an instrumentality are constantly subject to negotiation between and among various organs of state law and a variety of communities leads quickly to the position that not everything meaningful to investigate about "law" is found in the state. In a probing and rich essay, "Geography and Law: A Political Economy Perspective," Vera Chouinard has called upon geographers to reach beyond a "state-centered" approach to geographic work on law to adopt a "society-centered" methodology that emphasizes struggles over the form of law, a conjunctural theory of state, the formation of different subjectivities, and the variation of law over space.[46] She does not, however, abandon the notion that law is exclusively the product of the state (however negotiated) or adopt the position that other manner of social ordering might be dignified with that term.[47]

It seems to me that there is value in going this extra step. Social theorists such as Ehrlich and Selznick, whose views I touched upon above, offer definitions of "law" that include considerably more than the rules decreed by the state, and it seems logical to follow their lead in this respect. The most casual of comparative studies would quickly reveal that matters within the ambit of state regulation in some societies are left to private ordering in others but that this particular classification in no way implies anything about the total quantum of regulation. If it is at least partly true that law is about social directives — perhaps in some relationship to legitimating discourses — it is apparent that not all significant social directives or discourses originate in legislatures and courts. Social control, discursive engagement, and cooperative community organization may — but need not necessarily — take place through the organs of the state. No analysis can be complete without recognition of many levels of "legality" — or what I term here "legal pluralism." While a number of geographers and lawyers have recently expressed opinions on the desirable path of future research on law and geography, this dimension has unfortunately been largely overlooked. This is so despite long-standing recognition among legal scholars that law must be considered "in context" and that legal inquiry must extend beyond "law in the books."[48] Outside of the law and geography area, work in a legal pluralist vein has been both impressive and intellectually compelling[49] and it would be presumptuous, in the space of a short "perspective" chapter, to attempt exhaustively to set out the research agendas that might or should be pursued in light of insights to be derived from the perspective of legal pluralism.

The potential for this sort of research might, however, be illustrated by reference to two recent articles that address widely different applied issues. Matthews and Phyne paint a vivid portrait of the interaction between community "law" and state law with regard to Canadian inshore fisheries. The piece provides an excellent illustration both of the virtues of a committed "legal pluralist" approach and of the dangers of taking state law too seriously![50] Following Sabetti,[51] they contrast a Hobbesian "command theory of the rule of law," in which "a single over-arching structure of government arrangements is presumed to serve the public interests of all citizens,"[52] with a Tocquevillian-republican "democratic theory of the rule of law," which "emphasizes the possibility and importance of the self-governing community."[53] Applying these notions to the study of common resources, the authors invoke "democratic" (pluralist) notions of the rule of law to call into question Garrett Hardin's famous theorization[54] that imposed limits are needed in the management of finite common resources because otherwise "the pursuit of individual interests . . . produces collective irrationality."[55]

While Canadian fisheries law is premised on this Hobbesian view of common resources, Matthews and Phyne develop a specific, carefully constructed historical and empirical argument demonstrating that the "laws" that have always counted and that persist notwithstanding the existence of regulation by the state arise at the local level, derived from community cooperation and/or voluntary compliance.[56] State law and local "law" interact and ultimately, in this case, serve to reinforce each other, but it is local arrangement that governs the crucial question of who may fish by particular means in particular locations: "It is clear that, despite the instigation of licensing, traditional practices with regard to the local regulation of the commons continue to persist. They persist because licensing, as presently instituted, is little more than a labour management instrument controlling access to the fishery but not what occurs on the fishing grounds. Traditional cooperative arrangements remain because they do regulate the resource itself. That is, they are tools of resource management."[57] In short, researchers cannot begin to comprehend the fishery resource, the spatial economy from which it arises and that it supports, or the role of "law" in society and in space if state law is allowed to become the sole focus of investigation.

This conclusion is broadly supportive of a sense developed in other fields of sociolegal studies that social ordering is far more complex and multileveled than a simple investigation of "legal" doctrine would suggest.[58] It is also consistent with what Thrift calls "a situated or contextual epistemology, which acknowledges that people are historical, geographical and social beings."[59] Yet the method of Matthews and Phyne carries this epistemology further than has hitherto been the case in geographies of law by taking "context" beyond the state legal system and into the deeper "legalities" of human community.[60]

The Matthews and Phyne article is a useful illustration of the critical insights that might be obtained through the employment of an open-ended legal pluralism precisely because it demonstrates that even in developed capitalist legal (and economic) systems, the law of the state itself has no meaning when abstracted from other levels of legality. This is a profoundly important point, for we are not here concerned merely with a situation in which informal understandings fill in gaps or otherwise buttress the formal legal system. Rather, the article points out that the discourses and instrumentalities of state law are necessarily constituted in a dynamic relationship with other discourses, other "legalities," and other instrumentalities.

Another illustration of the utility of a "legal pluralism" approach is provided in a tightly woven analysis of the interplay of state law and customary law respecting land tenure in Kenya. In "Reconceptualizing Land Tenure Systems: Murang'a District, Kenya," Fiona Mackenzie addresses the thorny "problem of conceptualizing and defining the significance of "customary relations to land"[61] within a state legal system that explicitly takes account of customary (African) law of land tenure, transfer, succession, and inheritance.

An important starting point for Mackenzie, as for many researchers who find themselves drawn toward legal pluralism, is the recognition that formal law often fails to reflect what actually happens. Drawing on her own previous research[62] as well as that of others, Mackenzie concludes, with Homan, that formal law respecting land registration "was gradually ceasing to reflect the true state of affairs on the ground."[63] Specifically, she argues "that not only did the intersection between the two systems of tenure render rights to land insecure in general . . . but . . . the insecurity worked to the particular disadvantage of women."[64] She develops a sophisticated argument to the effect that in the Murang'a District, selective appeals to "customary" rights are "instrumental in increasing stratification in rural society" and that this has altered gender as well as class relations.[65]

Notwithstanding the importance of this conclusion; the view of law that is invoked in this piece is not a crude portrait of either an "instrument" or a code of "rules." Rather, Mackenzie emphasizes the mutability of both customary and state law in interaction with one another and in interaction with other discourses.[66] Rejecting both the views that customary law exists merely as an "imperial construct" and the contrary position that customary systems are "autonomous, ahistorical, the product of a self-contained particularity" she chooses to conceive of "customary law with respect to land tenure as a continuing domain of discourse. Here 'customary' rights to land, malleable and manipulable by individuals or groups, and thus subject to continual construction and reconstruction in the resolution of the conflict, become part of the process of legitimation of, frequently, individual material interest and thus social differentiation."[67] Despite the tendency toward increasing differentiation, it is important to note that the interplay of legal systems is identified as being subject to continuing reconstruction. As such, there is room for discourses of resistance: "The struggle over control of land is not completely one-sided."[68] Instead, "the nature of the interface between the two land tenure systems is seen not as determined by structural articulation, but as an arena of struggle where the actors are defined by class and gender."[69]

In sum, in Kenya as in maritime Canada, it is impossible even to begin to evaluate the social significance of either state law or less formal "legalities" without developing an analysis in which each sphere of "law" is assessed in its relationship to others. For Mackenzie, as for Matthews and Phyne, the discourses and instrumentalities of state law are necessarily constituted and reconstituted in a dynamic relationship with other discourses, other "legalities," and other instrumentalities. No adequate appreciation of the human environment, of spatial relations, of areal patterns can be developed if the complexities and multiple levels of analysis that this points to are glossed over.

CONCLUSION

It can be seen that there is tremendous potential for developing geographies of law at any number of levels and utilizing all conceivable types of geographical analysis. It is crucial, however, that geographers approaching the study of "geojurisprudence" not follow the lead of lawyers in artificially limiting their vision of the "legal" in ways that cut off rather than open up whole fields of inquiry. Geography can serve to enhance the development of research agendas in legal scholarship and not just play the role of "finding" the answers to empirical problems lawyers might define as important. We lawyers have all too strong a tendency to turn social scientists into our subordinates rather than equal partners in the development and execution of research projects. The greatest service that geographers can render to the broad field of interdisciplinary legal scholarship is, perhaps, to refuse to defer too much to "legal expertise" in formulating research agendas concerning the social world![70]

NOTES

1.   H.L.A. Hart, *The Concept of Law* (Oxford: Clarendon Press, 1961), 16.

2.   Roger Cotterell, *The Sociology of Law: An Introduction* (London: Butterworths, 1984).

3.   Sir George Stephen, as quoted in *Report of the Select Committee on Legal Education,* 25 August 1846, xxxv–xxxvi.

4.   Ibid., xlvii.

5.   For a general discussion, see Lawrence Ritt, "The Victorian Conscience in Action: The National Association for the Promotion of Social Sciences, 1857–1886" (Ph.D. Dissertation, Columbia University, 1959).

6.   The intellectual history of this movement remains to be adequately traced. Suggestive hypotheses are, however, to be found in Magali Sarfatti Larson, *The Rise of Professionalism: A Sociological Analysis* (Berkeley: University of California Press, 1977); Burton J. Bledstein, *The Culture of Professionalism: The Middle Class and the Development of Higher Education in America* (New York: W. W. Norton, 1978); Robert Stevens, *Law School: Legal Education in America from the 1850's to the 1980's* (Chapel Hill: University of North Carolina Press, 1983); David Sugarman, "Is the Reform of Legal Education Hopeless? or, Seeing the Hole instead of the Doughnut," *Modern Law Review,* 48 (1985): 728–736; David Sugarman, "Legal Theory, the Common Law Mind and the Making of the Textbook Tradition," in W. Twining (ed.), *Legal Theory and Common Law* (Oxford: Basil Blackwell, 1986); Morton J. Horwitz, *The Transformation of American Law, 1780–1860* (Cambridge: Harvard University Press, 1977). I have discussed these issues in more depth in W. Wesley Pue, "Guild Training vs. Professional Education: The Law Department of Queen's College, Birmingham in the 1850's," *American Journal of Legal History* (July 1989): 241–287. A comparative discussion of the "closing" of the Quebec legal mind is to be found in David Howes, "Dialogical Jurisprudence," in W. Wesley Pue and Barry Wright (eds.), *Canadian Perspectives on Law and Society: Essays in Legal History* (Ottawa: Carleton University Press, 1988).

7.   See, for example, Duncan Kennedy, "Toward an Historical Understanding of Legal Consciousness: The Case of Classical Legal Thought in America, 1850–1940," *Research in Law and Sociology,* 3 (1980): 3–24; Stevens, *Law School;* G. Edward White, "From Sociological Jurisprudence to Realism: Jurisprudence and Social Change in Early Twentieth–Century America," *Virginia Law Review,* 59, 2 (1972); reproduced in

White, *Patterns of American Legal Thought* (Indianapolis: Bobbs–Merrill, 1978), 99–135; Allan C. Hutchinson, "The Rise and Ruse of Administrative Law and Scholarship," *Modern Law Review,* 48 (1985): 293–324; Sugarman, "Legal Theory, the Common Law Mind and the Making of the Textbook Tradition."

8. Gregory S. Alexander, "The Transformation of Trusts as a Legal Category, 1800–1914," *Law and History Review,* 5 (1987): 303–350; Thomas C. Grey, "Langdell's Orthodoxy," *University of Pittsburgh Law Review,* 45, 1 (1983): 1–53; Robert Gordon, "Legal Thought and Legal Practice in the Age of American Enterprise, 1870–1920," in Gerald L. Geison (ed.), *Professions and Professional Ideologies in America, 1730–1940* (Chapel Hill: University of North Carolina Press, 1984); Sugarman, "Legal Theory, the Common Law Mind and the Making of the Textbook Tradition."

9. Oliver Wendell Holmes, "The Path of the Law," *Harvard Law Review,* 10, 457 (1897): 469.

10. See Laura Kalman, *Legal Realism at Yale, 1927–1960* (Chapel Hill: University of North Carolina Press, 1986); John H. Schlegel, "American Legal Realism and Empirical Social Science: From the Yale Experience," *Buffalo Law Review,* 28 (1979): 459–586; John H. Schlegel, "Between the Harvard Founders and the American Legal Realists: The Professionalization of the American Law Professor," *Journal of Legal Education,* 35 (1985): 311–325; Calvin Woodward, "The Limits of Legal Realism: An Historical Perspective," in H. P. Packer and T. Ehrlich (eds.), *New Directions in Legal Education* (New York: McGraw–Hill, 1972); Stevens, *Law School.*

11. See, for example, Peter Russell, "Overcoming Legal Formalism: The Treatment of the Constitution, the Courts and Judicial Behaviour in Canadian Political Science," *Canadian Journal of Law and Society,* 1 (1986): 5–34.

12. An extremely helpful review essay regarding the contribution of sociologists to developing workable paradigms as to the nature of "law" is Robert M. Rich, "Sociological Paradigms and the Sociology of Law: An Overview," in Charles Reasons and Robert Rich (eds.), *The Sociology of Law: A Conflict Perspective* (Toronto: Butterworths, 1978). I have relied greatly on that essay and on the pioneering collection in which it appeared in developing this chapter. Equally helpful with regard to political economy perspectives in Canada is Amy Bartholomew and Susan Boyd, "Toward a Political Economy of Law," in Wallace Clement and Glen Williams (eds.), *The New Canadian Political Economy* (Kingston: McGill–Queen's University Press, 1989), 212–239.

13. Talcott Parsons, "The Law and Social Control," in William E. Evan (ed.), *Law and Society* (New York: Free Press, 1962), 56–59, as paraphrased in Rich, "Sociological Paradigms and the Sociology of Law."

14. Philip Selznick, "The Sociology of Law," in Rita J. Simon (ed.), *The Sociology of Law* (Scranton, Pa.: Chandler, 1968); Philip Selznick, "The Sociology of Law," *International Encyclopedia of the Social Sciences* (New York: Free Press, 1968), paraphrased in Rich, "Sociological Paradigms and the Sociology of Law," 158–159.

15. P. H. Partridge, "Ehrlich's Sociology of Law," in Geoffrey Sawer (ed.), *Studies in the Sociology of Law* (Canberra: Australian National University, 1961), 5–7, as paraphrased in Rich, "Sociological Paradigms and the Sociology of Law," 151.

16. John Austin defined law as consisting mainly of commands in "The Province of Jurisprudence," *Lectures on Jurisprudence,* 1 (London: John Murray, 1911), 79; Hart, in *The Concept of Law,* 77–78, 80, took exception to this as amounting to no more than "the gunman situation writ large," while U.S. legal scholar Lon Fuller brilliantly spoofed this notion in *The Morality of Law* (New Haven: Yale University Press, 1969).

17. Parallel problems of boundary delimitation occur with attempts to define "state." See, for example, Perry Anderson's analysis of Antonio Gramsci's attempts in "The Antinomies of Antonio Gramsci," *New Left Review,* 100 (November 1976–January 1977): 5–80; Maureen Cain, "Gramsci, the State and the Place of Law," in David Sugarman (ed.), *Legality, Ideology and the State* (London: Academic Press, 1983), 95–118.

18. For a general account of these developments with particular reference to their impact on research and writing in legal history, see Barry Wright, "An Introduction to Canadian Law in History," in Pue and Wright, *Canadian Perspectives on Law and Society,* 7–19.

19. See, for example, Antonio Gramsci, *Selections from Prison Notebooks,* edited and translated by Quintin Hoare and Geoffrey Nowell Smith (London: Lawrence & Wishart, 1971); C. Buci–Glucksmann, *Gramsci and the State* (London: Lawrence & Wishart, 1980); Cain, "Gramsci, the State and the Place of Law"; Patricia Marchak, *Ideological Perspectives on Canada,* 2nd edition (Toronto: McGraw–Hill Ryerson, 1981); Sugarman, *Legality, Ideology, and the State;* Alan Hunt, "The Ideology of Law: Advances and Problems in Recent Applications of the Concept of Ideology to the Analysis of Law," *Law and Society Review,* 11 (1985): 11–37; Steve Brickey and Elizabeth Comack, "The Role of Law in Social Transformation: Is a Jurisprudence of Insurgency Possible?" *Canadian Journal of Law and Society,* 2 (1987): 97–119; Paul Hirst, *On Law and Ideology* (London: Macmillan, 1979); Colin Sumner, *Reading Ideologies: An Investigation Into the Marxist Theory of Ideology and Law* (London: Academic Press, 1979); Greg Marquis, "Doing Justice to 'British Justice': Law, Ideology and Canadian Historiography," in Pue and Wright, *Canadian Perspectives on Law and Society;* 43–70; Shelley Gavigan, "Women, Law, and Patriarchal Relations," in Neil Boyd (ed.), *The Social Dimensions of Law* (Scarborough: Prentice Hall Canada, 1986), 101–124; Shelley Gavigan, "Law, Gender and Ideology," in Anne Bayefsky (ed.), *Legal Theory Meets Legal Practice* (Edmonton: Academic Printing and Publishing, 1988). See also the special issue of *Law and Society Review,* 22, 4 (1988) on law and ideology.

20. See, for example, Peter Gabel and Paul Harris, "Building Power and Breaking Images: Critical Legal Theory and the Practice of Law," *New York University Review of Law and Social Change,* 11 (1982–1983): 369–411.

21. Phil Harris, *An Introduction to Law,* 3rd edition (London: Weidenfeld and Nicolson, 1988), 29.

22.   See, for example, "A Symposium: The Public/Private Distinction," *University of Pennsylvania Law Review,* 30 (1982); Nikolas Rose, "Beyond the Public/Private Division: Law, Power and the Family," *Journal of Law and Society,* 14 (1987): 61–76; Gerald Turkel, "The Public/Private Distinction: Approaches to the Critique of Legal Ideology," *Law and Society Review,* 22 (1988): 801; Peter Swan, "Critical Legal Theory and the Public/Private Distinction," Jurisprudence Centre, Working Paper, Carleton University, Ottawa, 1988.

23.   For a brief discussion, see W. Wesley Pue, "Issues in Social Welfare and Labour Relations," in Pue and Wright, *Canadian Perspectives on Law and Society,* 151–155 (and, generally, part 3 of that collection, pp. 150–242). A monumental U.S. book on legal history is largely concerned with these sorts of issues: Morton Horwitz, *The Transformation of American Law, 1780–1860* (Cambridge: Harvard University Press, 1977). There is, of course, nothing astonishingly "new" in the recognition that "private" law has public consequences. Max Weber, for example, observed that contract law is "accessible only to the owners of property and thus in effect supports their very autonomy and power positions"; Max Weber, *Max Weber on Law in Economy and Society,* edited by Max Rheinstein (Cambridge: Harvard University Press, 1966), 189. Friedrich Engels had earlier drawn attention to the coercive reality between formally noncoercive labor contracts in *The Origin of the Family, Private Property, & the State* (New York: International Publishers, 1942), 64, and in *The Condition of the Working Class in England* (New York: Macmillan, 1958).

24.   Hence, work such as Stuart Henry, *Private Justice: Toward Integrated Theorizing in the Sociology of Law* (London: Routledge and Kegan Paul, 1983).

25.   The work of Michel Foucault has been crucially important with respect to these developments, as has a good deal of scholarship originating in literary theory. Important texts include: Michel Foucault, *Discipline and Punish: The Birth of the Prison* (New York: Vintage, 1979); Michel Foucault, *Power/Knowledge,* Colin Gordon (ed.), Colin Gordon, Leo Marshall, John Mephal, Kate Soper (trans.) (New York: Pantheon Books, 1980). J. B. Thompson, *Studies in the Theory of Ideology* (Cambridge: Polity Press, 1984); Gary Peller, "The Metaphysics of American Law," *California Law Review,* 73 (1985): 1151–1290; Christopher Norris, *Deconstruction: Theory and Practice* (London: Methuen, 1982); Jonathan Culler, *On Deconstruction: Theory and Criticism After Structuralism* (London: Routledge and Kegan Paul, 1983); Allan C. Hutchinson, "From Cultural Construction to Historical Deconstruction," *Yale Law Journal,* 94 (1984): 209–237; Diane Macdonell, *Theories of Discourse: An Introduction* (Oxford: Basil Blackwell, 1986). For an insightful review of the receipt of literary theory by one important legal theorist, see Alan Hunt, "Living Dangerously on the Deconstructive Edge: A Review of *Dwelling on the Threshold* by Allan Hutchinson," *Osgoode Hall Law Journal,* 26 (1988): 867–895.

26.   Among recent studies in a legal pluralist vein, see Peter Fitzpatrick and Alfred Ruegg, review of *Without the Law: Administrative Justice and Legal Pluralism in Nineteenth–Century England,* by H. W. Arthurs, *Journal of Legal Pluralism,* 27 (1988): 135–143; Peter

Fitzpatrick, "Marxism and Legal Pluralism," *Australian Journal of Law and Society,* 1 (1983): 45–59; Peter Fitzpatrick, "Law, Plurality, and Underdevelopment," in Sugarman, *Legality, Ideology and the State,* 159–182; H. W. Arthurs, *"Without the Law': Administrative Justice and Legal Pluralism in Nineteenth–Century England* (Toronto: University of Toronto Press, 1985); H. W. Arthurs, "Special Courts, Special Law: Legal Pluralism in 19th Century England," in G. R. Rubin and David Sugarman (eds.), *Law, Economy and Society: Essays in the History of English Law, 1750–1914* (Abingdon: Professional Books, 1984); Henry, *Private Justice.* See also Leopold Pospisil, *Anthropology of Law: A Comparative Theory* (New York: Harper and Row, 1971); M. B. Hooker, *Legal Pluralism: An Introduction to Colonial and Neo–Colonial Laws* (Oxford: Clarendon Press, 1975); Antony Allott and Gordon R. Woodman (eds.), *People's Law and State Law: The Bellagio Papers* (Dordrecht: Foris Publications, 1985). Excellent review essays are Sally Engle Merry's "Legal Pluralism," *Law and Society Review,* 22 (1988): 869–896; John Griffiths, "What Is Legal Pluralism?" *Journal of Legal Pluralism,* 24 (1985): 1–55; and David Nelken, review essay, "Beyond the Study of 'Law and Society'" — Henry's *Private Justice* and O'Hagan's *The End of Law?" American Bar Foundation Research Journal* (1986): 323–338.

27. The hegemonic pretensions of lawyers are reflected in an old and well-known adage that in sociolegal research the social sciences should be "on tap, not on top."

28. See Ronald Dworkin, *Law's Empire* (London: Fontana, 1986), especially chapter 11, "Law Beyond Law."

29. On the notion of "boxes" that constrain intellectual inquiry regarding law, see R. W. Gordon, "J. Willard Hurst and the Common Law Tradition in American Legal Historiography," *Law and Society Review,* 10 (1975): 9; R. W. Gordon, "Historicism in Legal Scholarship," *Yale Law Journal,* 90 (1981): 1017; R. W. Gordon, "Critical Legal Histories," *Stanford Law Review,* 36 (1984): 57; David Flaherty, "Writing Canadian Legal History: An Introduction," in David Flaherty (ed.), *Essays in the History of Canadian Law,* vol. 1 (Toronto: Osgoode Society, 1981), 3–42; Barry Wright, "An Introduction to Canadian Law in History," in Pue and Wright, *Canadian Perspectives on Law and Society,* 7. To similar effect, and in specific reference to Hart and Dworkin, Alan Hunt distinguishes between "internal" and "external" legal theory: Alan Hunt, "The Critique of Law: What Is 'Critical' About Critical Legal Theory," *Journal of Law and Society,* 14 (1987): 5–20.

30. Dworkin, *Law's Empire,* 410.

31. Dworkin is much relied upon to assist in defining "law" even in the best work in the law-geography field. Examples include Nicholas K. Blomley, "Interpretive Practices, the State and the Locale," in Jennifer Wolch and Michael Dear, *The Power of Geography: How Territory Shapes Social Life* (Boston: Unwin Hyman, 1989); Nicholas K. Blomley, "Legal Interpretation: The Geography of Law," *Tijdschrift voor Economische en Sociale Geografie,* 78 (1987): 265; Gordon L. Clark and Michael Dear, *State Apparatus: Structures of Language and Legitimacy* (Boston: Allen and Unwin, 1984).

32. Risa Palm, "What Is Geography?" in Chapter 1 of this book.

33. Nicholas K. Blomley, "Geography and Law; Law and Geography," paper presented at the annual meeting of the Canadian Law and Society Association, Windsor, Ontario, June 7–9, 1988.

34. Nor is there any reason to artificially limit "impact studies" to contemporary research. Historical "jurisgeography" in this vein holds forth great promise. See, for example, Audrey Kobayashi, "From Tyranny to Justice: The Uprooting of Japanese Canadians After 1941," *Tribune Juive*, 5 (1987): 28–35; Audrey Kobayashi, "The Law as Justification of Spatial Tyranny: A Case Study of Japanese Canadians," paper presented at the annual meeting of the Canadian Law and Society Association, Windsor, Ontario, June 7–9, 1988.

35. M. B. Teitz, "Law as a Variable in Urban and Regional Analysis," *Papers of the Regional Science Association*, 41 (1978): 29–41.

36. Clark and Dear, *State Apparatus*, 104.

37. Debate in this area rages. For a useful review essay, see David Sugarman and G. R. Rubin, "Toward a New History of Law and Material Society in England 1750–1914" in Rubin and Sugarman, *Law, Economy, & Society*, 1–123. Law-capitalism relationships are sketched out — though not in a specifically geographical treatment — in Bartholomew and Boyd, "Toward a Political Economy of Law."

38. Feminist research has been particularly fruitful in shaking preconceptions in both law and geography. See Susan B. Boyd and Elizabeth Sheehy, "Canadian Feminist Perspectives on Law," *Journal of Law and Society*, 13 (1986): 283–320. Any issue of the *Canadian Journal of Women and the Law* also provides a handy point of reference in relation to feminist research and legal studies. With regard to feminist geography, see the report of the Women and Geography Study Group of the Institute of British Geographers, *Geography and Gender: An Introduction to Feminist Geography* (London: Hutchinson, 1984).

39. See, for example, Gordon L. Clark, "Law and the Interpretive Turn in the Social Sciences," *Urban Geography*, 10 (1986): 209–228; Gordon L. Clark, *Judges and the Cities: Interpreting Local Autonomy* (Chicago: University of Chicago Press, 1985). The impact of literary theory on legal scholarship has been immense. See note 26 above for a few references.

40. For example, Clark and Dear, *State Apparatus*.

41. For example, Gerald E. Frug, "The City as a Legal Concept," *Harvard Law Review*, 93 (1980): 1059–1154. See also Clark, *Judges and the Cities*.

42. Two articles by Josiah A.M. Cobbah eloquently argue for a geographically sensitive reevaluation of both the notion of sovereignty and of Western conceptions of the individual-group-state nexus: Josiah A.M. Cobbah, "Toward a Geography of Peace in Africa: Redefining Sub-State Self-Determination Rights," in R. J. Johnston, David Knight, and Eleonore Kofman, *Nationalism, Self-Determination and Political Geography* (London: Croom Helm, 1988), 70–86; Josiah A.M. Cobbah, "African Values and the Human Rights Debate: An African Perspective," *Human Rights Quarterly*, 9 (1987): 309–331. A helpful law and geography bibliography relating to sovereignty and self-determination is David B.

Knight and Maureen Davies, *Self-Determination: An Interdisciplinary Annotated Bibliography* (New York: Garland Publishing, 1987).

43.   For example, S. Mackenzie, "Women and the Reproduction of Labour Power in the Industrial City," Urban and Regional Studies, Working Paper 23, University of Sussex, Brighton, 1980; S. Mackenzie and D. Rose, "Industrial Change, the Domestic Economy and Home Life," in J. Anderson, S. Duncan, and R. Judson (eds.), *Redundant Spaces? Social Change and Industrial Decline in Cities and Regions* (London: Academic Press, 1983).

44.   See, for example, the historical work of Tom Johnson, "In a Manner of Speaking: Toward a Reconstitution of Property in Mid-Nineteenth Century Quebec," *McGill Law Journal,* 32 (1987): 636–672; Alan Pred, "The Social Becomes the Spatial, the Spatial Becomes the Social: Enclosures, Social Change and the Becoming of Places in Skåne," in Derek Gregory and John Urry (eds.), *Social Relations and Spatial Structures* (London: Macmillan, 1985), 337–365; Alan Pred, *Place, Practice and Structure: Social and Spatial Transformation in Southern Sweden, 1750–1850* (Cambridge: Polity Press, 1986); and the highly important work of Fiona Mackenzie, "Reconceptualizing Land Tenure Systems: Murang'a District, Kenya," paper prepared for the annual conference of the Canadian Association of African Studies, Queen's University, Kingston, May 11–14, 1988.

45.   Kim Economides, and Mark Blacksell called for this sort of work in "Law and Geography," *Journal of Law and Society,* 13 (1986): 161–182, subsequently published as "Human Geography and Law: A Case of Separate Development in Social Science," *Progress in Human Geography,* 10 (1986): 371–396. The Ph.D. dissertation of Jeroen Wagendorp at the University of Oklahoma represents an exhaustively researched attempt to "link culture and legal culture" (see Chapter 8, 136–148).

46.   Vera Chouinard, "Geography and Law: A Political Economy Perspective," paper presented at the annual meeting of the Canadian Law and Society Association, Windsor, Ontario, June 7–9, 1988.

47.   To similar effect, Bartholomew and Boyd adopt the position that "a developed political economy of law must explore and explain how complex and often contradictory material and social forces may 'determine' the emergence, change and direction of the form and content of laws and legal systems"; Bartholomew and Boyd, "Towards a Political Economy of Law," 216.

48.   See Phil Harris, "Approaches to the Teaching of Law Through Social Science Perspectives," Jurisprudence Centre Working Paper, Carleton University, Ottawa, 1985, esp. 6, 15.

49.   In addition to the works cited above, see, for example, Allott and Woodman, *People's Law and State Law; Proceedings of the Symposium on Folk Law and Legal Pluralism* 11th International Congress of Anthropological and Ethnological Studies, Harold W. Finkler (comp.) (Ottawa, Ontario, Office of Northern Research and Science Advisor, Indian and Northern Affairs, 1983); Fitzpatrick, "Marxism and Legal Pluralism"; Marc

Galanter, "Justice in Many Rooms," *Journal of Legal Pluralism*, 19 (1981): 1; Griffiths, "What Is Legal Pluralism?"; Merry, "Legal Pluralism." The *Journal of Legal Pluralism* is entirely dedicated to work in this vein.

50. Ralph Matthews and John Phyne, "Regulating the Newfoundland Inshore Fishery: Traditional Values Versus State Control in the Regulation of a Common Property Resource," *Journal of Canadian Studies*, 23 (1988): 158–176.

51. Filippo Sabetti, "Community Self Help and the Law and Regulations of Government," unpublished paper prepared for Liberty Fund Seminar on the Concept of Community and the Problem of Power, Niagara-on-the-Lake, Ontario, April 25–28, 1985.

52. Matthews and Phyne, "Regulating the Newfoundland Inshore Fishery," 160.

53. Ibid.

54. Garrett Hardin, "The Tragedy of the Commons," *Science*, 162 (1968): 1243–1248. Matthews and Phyne also address the similar arguments of H. Scott Gordon, "The Economic Theory of a Common Property Resource: The Fishery," *Journal of Political Economy*, 62 (1954): 124–142.

55. Matthews and Phyne, "Regulating the Newfoundland Inshore Fishery," 159.

56. Ibid., 165–172.

57. Ibid., 168.

58. See, for example, Terence G. Ison, *The Forensic Lottery: A Critique on Tort Liability as a System of Personal Injury Compensation* (London: Staples Press, 1967); P. S. Atiyah, *Accidents, Compensation, and the Law*, 3d edition (London: Weidenfeld and Nicolson, 1980); Stewart Macauley, "Non-Contractual Relations in Business: A Preliminary Study," *American Sociological Review*, 28 (1963): 55; Stewart Macauley, "An Empirical View of Contract," *Wisconsin Law Review* (1985): 465–482; W. David Slawson, "Standard Form Contracts and Democratic Control of Lawmaking Power," *Harvard Law Review*, 84 (1971): 529–566; Marc Galanter, "Why the 'Haves' Come out Ahead: Speculation on the Limits of Legal Change," *Law and Society Review*, 9 (1974); Kai Hildebrandt, Brian McNeely, and Peter P. Mercer, "Windsor Small Claims Courts," *Windsor Yearbook of Access to Justice*, 2 (1982): 87–123; Christopher Axworthy, "Controlling the Abuse of Small Claims Courts," *McGill Law Journal*, 22 (1982): 48. See generally the symposium issue, "Law, Private Governance and Continuing Relationships," *Wisconsin Law Review* (1985).

59. Nigel Thrift, "Flies and Germs: A Geography of Knowledge," in Gregory and Urry, *Social Relations and Spatial Structures*, 366–403, at 397, as quoted in Blomley, "Legal Interpretation," 274.

60. The "deeper legalities" of human communities have been crucial to developing appreciation of the operation of law in times past. See, for example, Douglas Hay, "Property, Authority and the Criminal Law," in Douglas Hay, Peter Linebaugh, and E. P. Thompson (eds.), *Albion's Fatal Tree: Crime and Society in Eighteenth Century England* (London: Allen Lane, 1975); Foucault, *Discipline and Punish*. The approach here resonates

in many ways with the repeated emphasis in Gordon L. Clark's important scholarship on interpretive approaches, which rely on a "continual interplay between text, context, and symbolic signification"; "Law and the Interpretive Turn in the Social Sciences," 221. However, Clark adheres more rigorously to a law-nonlaw dichotomy than seems warranted. See, for example, Clark, *Judges and the Cities,* 206 ("Legal modes represent instances where customary practices break down.") and xii ("I utilize a state-centered mode of inquiry.").

61. Mackenzie, "Reconceptualizing Land Tenure Systems," 1.

62. Fiona Mackenzie, "Land and Labour: Women and Men in Agricultural Change, Murang'a District Kenya," Ph.D. Dissertation, University of Ottawa, 1986; Fiona Mackenzie, "Local Initiatives and National Policy: Gender and Agricultural Change in Murang'a District, Kenya," *Canadian Journal of African Studies,* 20 (1986): 377–401.

63. F. D. Homan, "Succession to Registered Land in African Areas in Kenya," *Journal of Local Administration Overseas,* 1 (1963): 49–54, at 50.

64. Mackenzie, "Reconceptualizing Land Tenure Systems," 2–3. See also Fiona MacKenzie, "Land and Territory: The Interface Between Two Systems of Land Tenure, Murang'a District, Kenya," paper presented at the Canadian Association of African Studies conference, University of Alberta, Edmonton, May 7–9, 1987.

65. Mackenzie, "Reconceptualizing Land Tenure Systems," 4–5.

66. Ibid., 5–14; 27–31; 38–42.

67. Ibid., 1.

68. Ibid., 4.

69. Ibid., 5. In another context I have argued that the notion of "arena of struggle," though an advance on cruder conceptualizations of social process, is itself a flawed metaphor. See W. Wesley Pue, "Rebels at the Bar: English Barristers and the County Courts in the 1850's," *Anglo-American Law Review,* 16 (1987): 303–352, at 317.

70. Nicholas K. Blomley, "Text and Context: Rethinking the Law-Space Nexus," *Progress in Human Geography,* 13, 4 (1989): 512–534.

3

GEOGRAPHIC IMPLICATIONS OF WATER LAW

JAMES N. CORBRIDGE JR.

Lawyers and geographers have many interests in common — far more, indeed, than current levels of shared research and writing between the two disciplines would suggest. Both are concerned with the hydrologic cycle and climatic conditions. Both strive to understand the relationships between water supply and human activities in particular climatic settings. Water users are impacted by, and themselves impact, the physical environment in ways that command the attention of both disciplines.

Recent trends in water demand and use point to the need for a closer functional relationship between geography and water law. Conjunctive use of surface water and groundwater requires a better understanding of the physical connection between these two resources — a connection not always accurately reflected in the legal system. The impact of land use on water conservation and quality is an emerging area of inquiry. The regulation of floodplain building and occupancy cannot be accomplished successfully without the data of the geographer. Finally, the emphasis on planning as a tool in water resource management provides an opportunity for the lawyer and lawmaker to benefit from the perspectives familiar to geographic inquiry.

How can geographers contribute to the study of law? Geographers are uniquely qualified to judge the suitability of particular legal regimes to the times and places in which they operate. Geography also provides an alternative perspective from which to evaluate the success of past and proposed legal doctrines or legislation. A useful example is Platt's incisive critique of federal coastal barrier protection legislation in the United States.[1]

The tools of geography are increasingly useful in developing new legislation and in formulating scientific evidence for litigation. For example, remote sensing and aerial photography techniques promise clearer insights into land, boundary, and other resource disputes. Geographic information systems provide a helpful analytic framework for land use assessment and planning. Geographers can make important contributions to the promulgation of laws and regulations.

They can also serve as critical expert witnesses in those settings, such as weather modification suits, where geographic testimony on customary precipitation patterns is essential to meeting the burden of proof for litigants.[2]

The impact of law on the work of the geographer is also important. The social geographer studying the effects of flooding on floodplain residents must work within the constraints imposed by floodplain zoning, building codes, and the requirements of legally mandated insurance. Studies of real estate transactions in such areas of high geographic hazard as earthquake fault zones are influenced by the disclosure requirements imposed by law on real estate agents and financial lenders.[3]

Such studies can, in turn, conclude that the problem is the absence of appropriate regulation, leading to remedial legislation prompted by geographic inquiry. In addressing the legal system, the geographer should not assume law to be an immutable feature of the institutional landscape. By examining models based on different regulatory assumptions, geographers can perform a significant social service by providing lawmakers with alternative perspectives on the potential impacts of legislation. In this chapter we examine the actual and potential interaction between law and geography in the context of American water law. We focus on the two basic doctrines of American water law, illustrating the issues with selected cases that highlight the possible interaction between law and geography.

WATER LAW IN THE UNITED STATES

The allocation of water rights in the United States is primarily a question of state law and is characterized by two contrasting legal theories. The riparian system, borrowed from England and prevalent in the humid eastern states, generally ties water use to the ownership of riparian land bordering a watercourse. The appropriation system, in contrast, is based on the premise of distinct ownership of land and water. The use of water is controlled by a strict priority system — first in time, first in right — based on the date an individual water right is "perfected" by application of the water to a beneficial use.

The appropriation system is found in the relatively arid states lying westward of the 100th meridian. Some states, including Oregon, Washington, and California, have elements of both riparianism and appropriation, although it is fair to say that in those mixed systems appropriation dominates. In virtually all states that use appropriation, the underlying system has been modified in one way or another by the state legislature. Commonly, a permit approach has been imposed, whereby an administrative agency has been given regulatory authority over the acquisition, use, and loss of water rights.

These legal regimes originated in the context of the use of water in surface watercourses. Groundwater, at one time considered too mysterious and unknown to legislate, has been regulated under a number of approaches. These have not necessarily been riparian or appropriative in nature. Nor are surface water and groundwater law necessarily parallel.

In recent years water law has been affected by several concerns. Pollution and deteriorating environmental quality have influenced the development of water law, while rising interest in water-related recreation has spawned a growth in disputes involving competing uses of the surface of watercourses. In this context the appropriation system, with its focus on off-stream, consumptive uses, has proven ineffective. A separate doctrine, built on concepts of reasonableness and stressing the navigability of a particular watercourse, has arisen to deal with surface problems.

RIPARIAN RIGHTS

The doctrine of riparian rights was brought to American law from English common law in the early nineteenth century. It has had its fullest legal development in the eastern states, where relatively humid conditions facilitated its application. Riparian principles were designed to allocate water between property owners who occupied land alongside streams. Water use was limited to those riparian landowners. Transfer of water to land away from the stream was not permitted. Because riparian water rights are usufructuary and tied to landownership, these rights need not be exercised in order to be perfected.

Where two or more uses come into conflict under the riparian system, disputes are settled under a reasonable use doctrine that compares the reasonableness of the competing uses. One analysis has suggested several factors in the reasonableness equation: (1) the purpose of the use; (2) the suitability of the use to the watercourse or lake; (3) the economic and social value of the use; (4) the extent and amount of the harm it causes; (5) the practicality of avoiding the harm by adjusting the use or method of use of one proprietor or the other; (6) the practicality of adjusting the quantity of water used by each proprietor; (7) the protection of existing values of water uses, land, investments, and enterprises; and (8) the justice of requiring the user causing harm to adjust the loss. It is quite common to resolve conflicts between owners of riparian property by reducing the water allocated to each of the competing users. This approach is often used when droughts or other natural and temporary water shortages occur.

Over the years the basic principles of the riparian doctrine have been modified by state legislatures and regulatory agencies. For example, transfers to nonriparian uses are now permitted in many cases. Normally, transfers require compensation to riparian landholders whose interest may be diminished. The holders of riparian rights to use water may also receive protection against interference with water quality, although reliance on statutes or regulations specifically dealing with water quality is far more common today.

Riparian water law is often concerned with the effects of landforms, climate, and stream channel processes. A 1955 Arkansas case, *Harris* v. *Brooks,* illustrates this point.[4] *Harris* involved a lake about 3 miles long and 300 feet wide. Farmers who irrigated rice fields with lake waters were sued by the owner of a lakeside fishing business that rented boats and equipment to visitors. The fishing interests sought a court order preventing the farmers from reducing the lake level to an extent that interfered with fishing. The Arkansas Supreme Court, adopting a riparian law approach to the problem, attempted to establish the point at which lowering the lake level by water withdrawals would be unreasonable. The court concluded that the "normal" level was the reasonable level and ordered a stop to withdrawals beyond that point.

This outcome, though it has the virtue of apparent precision, is ultimately unsatisfying. Assuming that "below normal" and "unreasonable" are the same, what do we mean by "normal"? Normal over what time period? What is the relationship between normal lake levels and the demands of irrigating farmers, fishing interests, or other potential users? The conflict cries out for the kind of analysis that geographers are uniquely equipped to provide.

Geography also has a role to play in the larger policy issues facing states with riparian water law systems. Water storage and municipal water supply facilities in New England, for instance, are somewhat unevenly distributed, arguably in response to the focus of riparian law on watersheds rather than political boundaries. The result is an uneven distribution of the effect of periodic regional droughts. Rational redistribution of water storage could be planned by linking natural water supply and artificial storage to water user density.

THE APPROPRIATION SYSTEM

The appropriation system is a creature of the American West. As the West was settled, miners and farmers soon recognized that riparian principles that tied water use to land alongside water bodies were ill suited to the arid conditions prevailing in most of the West. Agriculture, mining, and other profitable land uses required reliable water supplies, but the riparian principle could not guarantee them. Thus the western states rejected the riparian principle, and the appropriation system emerged in its place.

In order to perfect an appropriative water right, the user must, under the original doctrine, divert the water and apply it to a beneficial use without waste. Once perfected, the right acquires a priority that is strictly enforced, with each appropriator fully satisfied in order of priority — hence the familiar shorthand expression of first in time, first in right. In contrast to the riparian principle, water under the appropriation system is not shared in times of shortage. Instead, junior appropriators must do without.

Nor is there any requirement tying water use to particular land. On the contrary, water rights are often sold apart from land, and water is commonly transferred away from the watershed of origin. Over the years many large-scale water diversion projects have been completed. Some, including the construction of canals from the Owens Valley of California to the Los Angeles Basin, extend for hundreds of miles. Large transbasin diversions have potentially profound effects on ecosystems, populations, communities, and economies. Legally imposed limitations on such transfers, as a possible urban growth management tool, are of interest to geographers.

One especially interesting feature of appropriative rights concerns transfers of existing rights. When these occur, there is a requirement that juniors be protected from injury. The junior is entitled to the continuation of stream conditions as they existed when the junior appropriation was made. As a practical matter, this has resulted in transfers' being limited to the historical consumptive use, when necessary to prevent injury to juniors. For this reason, the concept of consumptive use, including the amount, timing, and location of return flows, is of great importance in the management of water rights under the appropriation system. The junior protection rule has had a significant impact on the free flow of water market transactions in the West.

Administration of water rights in most of the appropriation states has been turned over to state agencies. These organizations are charged with managing water under permit systems. The fundamental principles of the appropriation system, as modified by the legislature and interpreted by the courts, are maintained. The permitting agency rarely has jurisdiction over water quality as well as quantity. Typically, the functions are split between two state agencies. As a result, the appropriation system itself has not proved effective in addressing environmental considerations.

An interesting case illustrating appropriation principles, including the conjunctive use of surface water and groundwater, is *Cache La Poudre Water Users Association* v. *Glacier View Meadows*.[5] In this Colorado case, downstream senior appropriators objected to an upstream housing development that proposed to draw water from groundwater sources tributary to the stream supplying the seniors. According to Colorado law, surface water and tributary groundwater are recognized as interdependent and are subject to the same legal doctrine.

The senior appropriators claimed that junior withdrawals would detract from the water supply available to fulfill the senior rights, in direct derogation of the appropriation doctrine. The well drillers were operating under Colorado's concept of a "plan for augmentation," in this case by buying replacement water and using it to augment the stream, thus maintaining the seniors' normal supply. The case, in fact, tested the idea of an augmentation plan, whereby out-of-priority uses are allowed in return for physical alteration of flow regimes that make up for the difference. The seniors argued that the river system in question, the Cache La Poudre basin, was overappropriated (that is to say, there were more water rights perfected in the system than could be satisfied in a normal year) and that neither the negative effect of upstream well withdrawals nor the ameliorative effect of the release of replacement water could be measured with sufficient accuracy to assure protection of the seniors. The Colorado Supreme Court noted the inherent uncertainty of western water rights and implicitly encouraged the ingenuity of those who can find usable water within an overappropriated system.

Glacier View Meadows represents traditional protections afforded by the appropriation law system, tested by an augmentation plan seeking to optimize the use of existing water, in a setting involving the increasingly common conjunctive use of surface water and groundwater sources. Both augmentation and conjunctive use will require extensive reexamination in the years ahead. The question whether plans for augmentation, as contemplated under the water law of Colorado and other states, represent inappropriate imposition on the integrity of stream basin supplies has already been raised.

SURFACE USE OF WATERCOURSES

Because of the growth of water-based recreation in recent years, the use of waterways for boating, fishing, and hunting has increased. Along with increased recreational water use has come conflict with other users, as we already saw in the case of *Harris* v. *Brooks*.

Customary water law doctrines, which have been developed to deal primarily with consumptive uses, have yet to address surface use problems effectively. This has been particularly true in areas whose water law is based on the appropriation system, with its focus on off-stream consumptive uses. Even in these states, there has been a tendency to fall back on the reasonableness concepts associated with riparianism. Surface rights have been extended to the public at large by classifying certain waters as "navigable," while the right to use the surface of "nonnavigable" waters has been associated with ownership of the bottom of the watercourse.

In those waters considered navigable under the so-called federal test, title to the bottom generally was conveyed to the individual states at the time of statehood.[6] Even in waters where this is not true, some states have developed their own tests, extending navigability — and therefore public use of the surface — to waters not included under the federal test. Even where nonnavigable watercourses are involved, bottom ownership may be divided among several persons, raising issues about their common right to use the overall surface. Further conceptual difficulty is introduced where a watercourse is artificially created or expanded.[7]

The geographer can play an important role in helping to sort out the resources policy issues in this area of the law. It has long been clear that policy and management questions could not be solved by relying on the technicalities of water law.[8] Geographic analysis of the resource, its distribution, and the likely demands that will be put on it would be a useful step toward more effective legislation to guide the courts in allocating water recreation resources.

A related set of problems deals with the location of the surface area of watercourses. Many boundaries, including those of states themselves, are set according to the location of rivers, lakes, and streams. Private boundaries may change in accordance with changes in the location of the watercourse that defines them, under the legal doctrines of accretion and reliction. At least one geographer has noted the importance of these principles to geography.[9]

Some rivers — the Missouri is a notable example — are notorious for changing their courses, raising disputes over valuable property rights in the process.[10] These changes impact geography, and geographic tools, including aerial photography and remote sensing, are critical in establishing the location of old and new watercourses.

GROUNDWATER

Excessive demand on surface supplies and the invention of the submersible turbine pump have led, over nearly fifty years, to increased reliance on groundwater for human consumption, agriculture, industry, and many other uses, posing a challenge for our legal system, which must allocate groundwater resources.

The relationship between law and the realities of geography, hydrology, and economics is difficult. The unknowns of mysterious, underground water sources confounded the early courts, and the result was a confusion of legal approaches, not necessarily related to surface water doctrine, even in the same jurisdiction. This failure to recognize the basic interrelationship between surface water and groundwater was bound to create legal confusion. Only recently have courts and legislatures made a consistent effort to sort things out.

Several distinct approaches to groundwater law have been developed. The theory of absolute ownership grants control of underground waters to the surface owner. Under this approach a well driller could pump even if only to spite other landowners overlying the aquifer. In other cases a strict appropriation doctrine, with state-controlled permits required for any pumping, has been used. Between these extremes has been a welter of legal regimes, including modifications of the riparian reasonable use approach, correlative rights/proration, and such modified appropriation approaches as those of Colorado and Arizona.

In addition to resolving conflicts between competing groundwater users and between groundwater users and affected surface water users, legal systems have addressed the problem of groundwater mining or the withdrawal of groundwater at greater than annual recharge or safe yield rates. Policy concerns obviously have dominated such legislation, and mere protection of groundwater levels has not been the only policy consideration. Colorado's statute, for instance, contemplates the eventual lowering of groundwater in high plains aquifers below economically recoverable levels.

To the extent that groundwater legal systems regulate long-range water supplies in ways that set parameters on human activity in a particular area, they directly affect the thrust of geographic inquiry. So, too, can the perspectives and tools of geography affect the direction of legislation and the outcome of litigation. In the application of computer technology to measuring the effects of groundwater use, modeling has played an increasingly important role. Furthermore, the relationship between land use and groundwater quality, with its planning and legal implications, has been explored recently by a Swedish geographer.[11]

A case whose scope and complexity attract the attention of geographer, engineer, lawyer, and political scientist alike is *Alamosa-LaJara Water Users Protection Association* v. *Gould*.[12] The State of Colorado had fallen well behind in its legal obligation to deliver Rio Grande water to New Mexico and Texas under the terms of the Rio Grande Compact signed by the three states. These debits began accumulating in 1952; in 1966 New Mexico and Texas sued Colorado in the U.S. Supreme Court. By way of settlement, Colorado agreed to begin meeting its water delivery obligations, and the Colorado state engineer promulgated rules governing the delivery of water on the basis of projected annual runoff from the Rio Grande basin. These rules and their administration were challenged in the Colorado state courts by both ground- and surface water users along the Rio Grande. At issue was whose diversions would be shut down, in what priority, and to what extent, in order to provide Texas and New Mexico with water in times of inadequate basin runoff.

In addition to perplexing legal questions, this case involved hydrologic and administrative issues of great difficulty. Water users were located on Rio Grande tributaries as well as on the main stem. A complex interface existed between surface water and groundwater supplies. A significant groundwater aquifer was not materially connected to a surface stream. Those who had historically exercised private rights in a region where irrigation is essential to the agricultural economy were being ordered to stop pumping or diverting on behalf of a broader, public interest. The state engineer proposed that some surface water users be required to withdraw tributary groundwater in order to satisfy their rights. Under such circumstances a physical solution may be needed in addition to a legal one. Indeed, a physical solution — the Closed Basin Project — was in part used to resolve the issues in Alamosa-LaJara, by providing alternate nontributary groundwater supplies to meet Colorado's compact obligations. Physical solutions are an increasingly attractive approach in water law disputes.[13] Their effectiveness and availability raise questions far beyond the purely legal questions, demanding the expertise of the hydrologist, the engineer, and the geographer.

CHANGING LAW AND CHANGING GEOGRAPHY

Like geography, water law has undergone a considerable evolution in recent years. Part of this has been a response to changing disputes that reflect changing human activity, as with the increase of cases involving surface recreation and the conjunctive use of surface water and groundwater. In part, the change has been driven by technology. Developments in groundwater withdrawal (and injection) techniques and improved knowledge of aquifer location and behavior have contributed to greater use of groundwater and to the legal attention that inevitably follows. Attempts at weather modification, however primitive, have also spawned legislation and litigation.[14]

All of this is not surprising. Water law deals with a critical natural resource, has a close relationship to science and engineering, and addresses policy issues of enormous public interest. To the extent that the tools of science, including geography, become more sophisticated, their use in shaping water law is bound to increase.

The important policy issues associated with water use and availability also suggest that the geographer's interest is not limited to the concerns of the physical geographer. Water is an essential ingredient of the human condition. With water the deserts bloom; without it civilization ceases to flourish. Even in humid areas of the world, governmental action is required to provide the population with a dependable supply of potable water. In arid regions water supply is a critical element to virtually all human activity. The sociopolitical setting (of which the legal system is an important part) makes water more or less available as a resource — with great impact on the life of the local inhabitants. Location of land along watercourses has a significant effect on its value, both up and down. Governmental intervention to prevent or ameliorate flood damage to riparian property and those who inhabit it is common. These points raise important issues of concern to social and political geographers, as well as to water lawyers and lawmakers.

The celebrated geographer and water resources scholar Gilbert White has written that "the likelihood of the world running out of water for sustaining its life is zero; the likelihood grows of its grossly mismanaging its water resource unless the proper political and technological decisions are made."[15] The sound management of water resources will require the combined efforts of geographer and lawyer.

NOTES

1.   Rutherford H. Platt, Sheila G. Pelczarski, and Barbara K.R. Burbank (eds.) (1987), *Cities on the Beach: Management Issues of Developed Coastal Barriers*. Chicago: University of Chicago, Department of Geography, Research Paper 224.

2.   James N. Corbridge Jr. and Raphael J. Moses (1968), "Weather Modification: Law and Administration," *Natural Resources Journal*, 8, pp. 207–235.

3.   Risa Palm and James N. Corbridge Jr. (1982), "The Unintended Impacts of Anti-Redlining Legislation," *Journal of Environmental Systems*, 12, pp. 341–349.

4.   *Harris v. Brooks*, 225 Ark. 436, 283 S.W.2d. 129 (1955).

5.   *Cache La Poudre Water Users Association v. Glacier View Meadows*, 191 Colo. 53, 550 P.2d. 288 (1976).

6.   J. Frank (1982), "Forever Free: Navigability, Inland Waterways and the Expanding Public Interest," *University of California at Davis Law Review*, 16, pp. 579–629.

7.   James N. Corbridge Jr. (1984), "Surface Rights in Artificial Water Courses," *Natural Resources Journal*, 29, pp. 887–928.

8.   G. Graham Waite (1958), "The Dilemma of Water Recreation and a Suggested Solution," *Wisconsin Law Review*, pp. 542–609.

9.   Olen Paul Matthews (1984), *Water Resources, Geography and Law*. Washington, D.C.: Association of American Geographers.

10.   Robert E. Beck (1966), "The Wandering Missouri River: A Study in Accretion Law," *North Dakota Law Review*, 43, pp. 429–466; Laurie Smith Camp (1977), "Land Accretion and Avulsion: The Battle of Blackbird Bend," *Nebraska Law Review*, 56, pp. 814–835.

11.   Hans Lhonegren, *Control of Land Use and Groundwater Quality in Colorado and Sweden*, thesis, University of Linkhoping, Linkhoping, Sweden, 1987.

12.   *Alamosa-LaJara Water Users Protection Association v. Gould*, 674 P.2d. 914 (Colorado, 1983).

13.   Harrison C. Dunning, "State Equitable Apportionment of Western Water Resources," *Nebraska Law Review*, 66, pp. 76–119.

14.   Corbridge and Moses (1968).

15.   Gilbert White (1983), "Water Resource Adequacy: Illusion and Reality," *Natural Resources Forum*, 12.

4

WATER LAW AND GEOGRAPHY: A GEOGRAPHIC PERSPECTIVE

OTIS W. TEMPLER

Geographers have long been interested in the analysis of land and water use, but only in the past few years have they begun paying closer attention to the legal framework controlling the allocation of water supplies and water rights. Although the imprint of the institutions that control water allocation and use may not always be readily apparent, closer examination reveals their considerable importance.

Water rights law constrains how water is used. Once water law systems are established, they tend to resist change and are sometimes difficult to replace or modernize. As competition for limited water supplies increases, the water rights systems inherited from the past sometimes become notable obstacles to desirable water resource management reforms. What is more, water law systems can govern spatial patterns of cultural and economic development, thus having a significant impact on the resultant landscape. Ultimately, law is an important variable in understanding and explaining these patterns associated with water use.

Other important aspects of water law focus on the evolution and diffusion of water rights systems. Study of the evolution of water law provides evidence of a particular society's perception of its natural environment and water resources. The court decisions, statutes, administrative rules, and customary practices that form the basis of existing water law reflect a society's changing attitudes toward water and the extent and dependability of water supply. It is also possible to trace the cultural diffusion of these legal systems and the changes they have undergone in response to cultural and environmental realities.

Because of the great diversity of water law and water rights problems, the discussion in this chapter is limited and selective, focusing on the expanding interface of the two disciplines in water resources research. Thus it provides a summation of some of the important research themes and the contributions geographers and, to a lesser extent, lawyers have made to the analysis of water law problems. Examples drawn from my research on several water laws illustrate issues of concern to a broad spectrum of those involved with water law and water resource management. Finally, I comment on some inherent obstacles to effecting needed or desirable changes in water law and policy.

THE INTERFACE OF GEOGRAPHY AND WATER LAW

Many geographers realize the importance of assessing and analyzing the impact of institutional constraints on resource management. In 1965, in *The Science of Geography,* Ackerman pointed out what was then deemed to be an area of highly significant research, defining the problems of such studies as "the disequilibrium in a political system caused by non-conformities between land occupance [and resource use] and the existing legal system."[1] Even earlier, Whittlesey noted perceptively that "laws unsuited to regions where they operate ultimately destroy the resource which they govern."[2]

Since that time, a growing number of geographers have been actively involved in attempting to advance this research frontier. There are numerous examples in the literature of contributions by geographers analyzing the problems of water use, development, and management.[3] These studies have usually dealt with broad policy issues rather than specific water law and water rights problems. Hamming, however, has provided a more specific analysis of the spatial patterns of surface water law and the divergent riparian and prior appropriation doctrines in the United States.[4] Researchers have subsequently examined water rights issues pertaining to the hydrologic cycle, to water in each of the several phases of the cycle, to conjunctive management of interconnected water resources, and to the related problems of public access to surface water resources.[5]

From his relatively unique vantage point as a geographer-lawyer, Matthews has been especially important in making geographers more aware of "a small but growing body of literature linking geography and law as fundamental disciplines" and in identifying several research themes to which geographers might profitably contribute.[6] Among other notable recent contributions are studies of water rights problems pertaining to Colorado and the Colorado River basin and studies on the problem of groundwater depletion in the western states and its relationship to diverse legal principles applied to groundwater.[7] Nor are geographers alone in providing analyses of water law with spatial dimensions, especially noteworthy examples being the comparisons of water law regimes by Teclaff.[8]

Notwithstanding these significant advances, much research remains to be accomplished at the interface of geography and law. Ouellet attributes most water resource management problems to the large number of laws constraining water use and the multiplicity of water agencies that deal with various aspects of water use, often with little coordination among them. Goldfarb believes that optimum water resource policy can evolve only if all components of the water resource management field (physical, social-scientific, and legal-institutional) can be integrated into comprehensive analysis and decisionmaking.[9]

Despite the growing importance of in-stream water uses for recreation and environmental preservation, water law has traditionally been associated with human consumptive use of water, particularly diversions for economic uses. Thus water law involves the study of property concepts. Because water is a mobile resource, many traditional concepts of ownership and property rights are not entirely appropriate in water law. However, the role of law is critically important to water resource management because of the necessity of establishing order through clearly defined property rights and rules of liability. The degree of success of water law in allocating the resource among competing uses and users ultimately is measured by such considerations as stability (security, predictability) and flexibility (efficiency).[10]

As will be seen, the common law achieves stability by its reliance on precedent, where the courts follow previously established legal rules. Flexibility is attained by encouraging the courts to distinguish fact situations and by providing for changes in legal rules by the courts and legislatures. Matthews raises the question of how law should change.[11] Should new water laws be passed in anticipation of management problems, or does the law develop best when it responds to an already existing problem?

There is also conflicting opinion over how rapidly water law should evolve, representing as it does the "formalization" of water policy. Where the law on a subject is well developed, it usually changes slowly and only at the periphery. Getches describes how the courts and legislatures alter law in response to societal stimuli, with historical conditions controlling water law's initial development and then different modern circumstances compelling further change.[12] Goldfarb contends that the legal system is inherently conservative in that courts and legislatures are reluctant to overturn existing water law, with the result that much water law is based on outdated science, as will be illustrated by the subsequent discussions of the legal classifications of water and conjunctive management.[13]

Yet Getches considers water law to be a young and dynamic field — "an evolving field replete with conflicts over a critical resource possessing various tangible and intangible values [presenting] unparalleled opportunities for analysis and creativity."[14] The relative rate of change varies a great deal, of course, from state to state and also by the specific type of water law issue in question. Moreover, there is much contradictory policy at the local, state, and federal levels. Since each state has the power to regulate water use and create water rights, fifty different state water laws have evolved, with no two identical in all respects.

Because water law is often complex and much is specific to one jurisdiction, broad generalizations and comparisons concerning it can sometimes be misleading and erroneous, especially where subtle exceptions and nuances are ignored. Water law is often ambiguous, and only rarely is it clear and definitive, a point that nonlawyers find difficult to understand. Even if there is general agreement about a topic at one point in time, concepts change, requiring constant reinterpretation and reevaluation.[15]

Despite the expanding interface of law and geography, those not trained in the law cannot be expected to make accurate, detailed analyses of water law. That is the province of lawyers. Geographers can, however, by using the viewpoints and methodologies of their discipline, study the impact and effect of water law on opportunities for economic development and the spatial aspects and spatial variations in land and water use. Thus geographers can help legal scholars to critically evaluate the performance of existing law. They can also help provide supportive data and suggest solutions for unresolved water law problems. Goldfarb has noted that much of the legal literature is stylistically inaccessible to nonlawyers.[16] Lawyers can and often do provide analyses of complex water law problems in less intricate legal language, making geographers and other scholars and professionals involved in water resource management more aware of the numerous institutional constraints under which they must operate.[17]

WATER LAW AND THE HYDROLOGIC CYCLE

Nature's hydrologic cycle explains the movement of water. Because physical scientists recognize the unity of the hydrologic cycle, they generally view all water as merely passing through the different phases of the cycle. While they do distinguish between the phases (atmospheric moisture, surface water, soil water, and groundwater) for purposes of classification and study, they do not separate and assign each phase to permanent classes that do not exist in nature, and they recognize the interrelatedness of the various phases of the cycle.

In contrast, law governing different stages of the hydrologic cycle is often contradictory, with different laws developed to control each part of the cycle. The law divides water in the hydrologic cycle into several different classes, based on real or supposed differences in each class. Each legal class of water is treated separately, usually without recognition of the interrelationships existing within the cycle, and different rules of law have arisen concerning ownership and use of the various classes.[18]

The point at which water is diverted from its natural state and brought under human control determines the appropriate legal classification. This legal classification system has frequently been criticized because it is well known that there are often widespread interconnections between the various phases and also that human interference with water in one phase of the cycle can significantly affect opportunities for use and control at another point.[19] Thomas has referred to the legal classifications of water as "a lawyer's paradise and a logician's nightmare."[20]

He further contended that the hydrologic cycle provides a logical basis for distinction of private rights inherent in landownership as opposed to public rights subject to appropriation.[21] In fact, however, most water law precedents were established when scientific knowledge of the operation of the hydrologic cycle was much less detailed than today. Some rules, such as those of the English common law, were developed in physical environments quite different from those where they are currently being applied.

This system has made it difficult for the courts to recognize and apply current scientific knowledge. Thus the law reflects the understanding of hydrology and the perception of water resources at the time it developed, tending to perpetuate erroneous hydrologic notions that now make for inefficiency in water resource management. However illogical this obsolete legal classification system may seem, the courts of most states have divided water moving in the hydrologic cycle into the same legal classes. The failure of the law to recognize the unity of water in the various phases of the hydrologic cycle is blamed on the tendency of the courts to simplify and compartmentalize legal problems. Dolson also suggests that most lawsuits involving water are between claimants to the same legal class.[22] Legal classifications thus developed in the same way, with different rules of law for each class. Many of the problems resulting from the fragmentation of water rights in the hydrologic cycle are evident in the following example involving Texas water law.[23]

TEXAS WATER LAW

There are many questions concerning the right to atmospheric moisture in Texas.[24] A few states claim sovereign rights to clouds or atmospheric moisture, but Texas does not. However, Texas courts have perhaps gone farther than those of any other state in attempting to find private rights in atmospheric moisture, one appellate court opinion finding that the landowner is entitled "to such rainfall as may come from clouds over his own property that Nature, in her caprice may provide."[25] Despite increasingly strict state regulation of weather modification activities following passage of the Weather Modification Act in 1967, the question of relative private and public rights to atmospheric moisture remains unsettled in Texas.

Once precipitation has fallen and collected as sheet flow on the land surface, it becomes part of another legal classification, diffused surface water. It is generally established in Texas that landowners are entitled to intercept and use diffused surface water on their land, and this right is superior to that of adjacent lower landowners and of anyone who holds rights to surface water on streams into which the water might eventually flow.[26] The rule in Texas is similar to that of most other jurisdictions.[27] Interception of surface runoff by landowners can significantly impact existing downstream water rights, the owners of which have no legal recourse.

Upon reaching a stream course, water is subject to still other types of water rights. Texas, a dual-doctrine state, recognizes both the riparian doctrine — a complex blend of Hispanic civil and English common-law principles — and the prior appropriation doctrine for allocating surface water rights. With both doctrines present, numerous riparian and appropriative water rights exist side by side on most streams. Needless to say, state water agencies and water users have always had great difficulty in coordinating the diverse private and public water rights emanating from these diametrically different doctrines.[28] Only a recently completed adjudication of all surface water rights — begun in 1969 to merge all rights into the permit system — gives some promise of finally resolving this complex surface water management issue.[29]

Texas law is well settled with respect to percolating groundwater.[30] The strict common-law rule, established in 1904 in the landmark case of *Houston & T. C. Ry. Company* v. *East,* gives overlying landowners the right to groundwater beneath their land.[31] In general, a landowner can pump and use groundwater with few restrictions and with little regard for the effect on adjoining landowners or more distant users of groundwater or interconnected surface water. Local underground water conservation districts formed under a 1949 general law or by special legislation exercise about the only control over landowner rights, and Texas courts and the legislature have always been wary of infringing on these recognized private rights to underground water.

This discussion has shown that Texas water rights law is extremely fragmented, a veritable hodgepodge of competing and contrasting public and private rights, all of which make any efforts at unified and efficient administration and conservation difficult, if not impossible. In some states the water rights picture is much less complex than in Texas. Many states have abrogated the riparian doctrine and strict common-law groundwater rules; some other dual-doctrine states adjudicated surface water rights much earlier. Nevertheless, this example provides a microcosmic view of water rights problems stemming from the legal classifications of water, problems that have been experienced to varying degrees by most states.

CONJUNCTIVE MANAGEMENT OF WATER RESOURCES

The legal division of water rights in the various phases of the hydrologic cycle and problems preventing the conjunctive management of water resources are closely connected. "Conjunctive management," as used here, simply refers to the situation where water in two or more phases of the hydrologic cycle is managed as an integrated resource. It is generally agreed, considering the substantial interconnections between the phases of the hydrologic cycle, that conjunctive management is often a desirable objective, especially where it can be demonstrated that unregulated water use in one phase has appreciable effects on recognized water rights and opportunities for water use in other phases. It is thought that larger amounts of water can be made available for more efficient use through integrated management that considers the needs of the various users holding valid water rights, the nature and location of available water resources, and how existing uses can be managed to conserve water and reduce waste. Well-established interconnections are generally most evident for groundwater and surface water in streams, these two phases usually being the only ones considered in discussions of conjunctive use and management. However, atmospheric moisture and diffused surface water represent other important hydrologic phases that might someday be integrated with the other two, though conjunctive management involving them is rarely attempted.[32]

Despite its purported advantages, conjunctive management of water resources is practiced in only a few states, the chief barriers to its implementation being the existing state water law structure. One solution to achieving coordinated and more efficient management of water resources in Texas might be for the state to establish an all-inclusive appropriation system for application to water in whatever phase of the hydrologic cycle it might be found, thus effectively bringing the total water resource under unified control. Such a broad appropriation system would be most unusual, and the likelihood of establishing such an all-inclusive system is indeed remote. However, Thomas maintained that until this is done, correlation and management of water rights in all phases of the hydrologic cycle cannot be achieved, and problems in which water use in one phase affects water rights in other phases will continue to arise.[33] Earlier I noted how the courts failed to recognize prospective problems at the time the fragmented legal classifications of water evolved. State legislatures have also generally failed to consider the interrelated nature of water resources. Once this dual judicial-legislative legal system develops and becomes firmly established, it becomes even more difficult to find any definitive and immediate solution.[34]

In the western United States, conjunctive use has sometimes been instituted, often during periods of water crisis. The states most often cited as working examples of conjunctive management systems are New Mexico, Colorado, and California. Both Colorado and New Mexico apply the appropriation doctrine to surface water and underground water, and even here coordinated administration has not been entirely successful. Problems have been attributed to the deeply entrenched separate legal systems for one integrated water supply. California law is more closely analogous to Texas in that it applies both the riparian and appropriation systems to surface water and a variation of the common-law rule, correlative rights, to groundwater.[35]

Omitting any consideration of atmospheric moisture and diffused surface water, it is recognized that correlated water use and management in a dual-doctrine and common-law-rule state like Texas would be even harder to achieve.

Surface waters, appropriated by the state, can be managed in the general public interest, whereas groundwater is privately owned and is not subject to such control. The absolute ownership rule applied to groundwater provides no basis for correlating rights in an integrated supply. Thus the long-established legal division of water into discrete classes effectively bars conjunctive management of surface and underground water in Texas. The magnitude of recognized groundwater rights prevents extension of appropriation to groundwater, as it was earlier applied to surface water. Thirty years ago Hutchins pointed out that Texas court decisions had already welded the absolute ownership rule into a rule of property that would be most difficult to overturn.[36]

The institutional constraints of law and politics, though of paramount importance, are not the only obstacles to achieving conjunctive management of water resources. There is also a lack of specific data on the operation of the hydrologic cycle. The volumes of moisture moving through the various phases of the cycle are relatively constant on a world scale but are much more variable for any specific state or region, and in limited areas the quantities of water in each phase are subject to still more fluctuation. In only a few areas is there a reasonably complete and quantitative description of the operation of the cycle, and the resultant hydrologic uncertainties are said to present significant legal problems. Though it would appear that there are often adequate data available for stream flow and groundwater, there is less certain information on the combined resource. Some investigators maintain that there is not yet enough information available to allow the complete and efficient administration of conjunctive use.[37]

PROBLEMS OF IN-STREAM WATER USE

Water adequacy has usually been viewed almost exclusively in terms of off-stream water uses, often at the expense of in-stream requirements for fish and wildlife habitat maintenance and water-based recreation. In most states the primary emphasis has generally been directed toward achieving maximum beneficial use and full development of streams so that fresh water would not be "wasted." Now, however, as streams have become more fully regulated, or even overappropriated, there is a growing concern with maintaining minimum levels of flow for enhanced recreational use and fish and wildlife habitat protection and, in some coastal states, with providing sufficient freshwater inflow to protect the quality and resources of estuarine systems.[38]

Those concerned with river management and planning must reckon with water already appropriated as a part of the existing water rights situation. Even more important are future appropriations and unquantified or excessive appropriations. The impact on overappropriated streams may be mitigated somewhat if state or federal law provides minimum stream flow requirements or provides that creation of the system under which the river manager operates constitutes a reservation of the necessary water. Many investigators cite differences in trying to maintain in-stream flow depending on whether a state follows the riparian or the prior appropriation doctrine. Anderson summarizes many of the difficulties of establishing in-stream flow rights and the potential conflict with existing off-stream uses in states that apply prior appropriation.[39] Recognition of most in-stream uses, other than for navigation, are fairly recent. Stone notes that until the modern era, the public made little demand for the use of inland waters, other than for navigation and to a lesser extent for fisheries. Thus there has been little occasion for the law to consider expanded public use.[40]

If in-stream flow is available, in general the question of whether or not the recreation-seeking public can have access to streams turns on issues of navigability and streambed ownership. The English tidewater test of navigability was rejected in the United States. Instead, a test of "navigability in fact" was adopted, so that all coastal and inland waters are subject to public use if they are capable of supporting navigation. Federal court decisions establish the legal test of navigability for state ownership, then each state may declare its own legal test of navigability for the purpose of establishing the public trust and rights of public use of its waters. Most states have adopted tests for navigability for inland waters akin to the federal test, but a number of variations have been developed by the states to expand the relatively narrow federal definition of commercial navigability.[41] The National Water Commission explained why case law on the public access question has not developed rapidly in this country: "Many of the legal questions relating to navigability and the public trust are extremely complicated and must be resolved by the judiciary."[42]

There is considerable variation from jurisdiction to jurisdiction, making generalizations and comparisons difficult, and there are a number of unique situations. Thus much of the law of public access and in-stream water use is still evolving. Johnson and Austin have observed that differences among the states concerning surface use of streams and lakes, such as for recreation, do not correlate well with the notable differences in consumptive water use, which basically relates to the application of the prior appropriation doctrine in the western states and the riparian doctrine in the eastern states.[43]

In most eastern states, an inland stream must be navigable in fact for the public right of access and enjoyment to be asserted, though the rationale supporting this rule varies considerably from state to state. The effect is to give the nonriparian public a share in the use and enjoyment of a river or stream that otherwise might be largely monopolized by private riparian owners. The nature and extent of permitted uses and the criteria for designating streams as navigable vary markedly, resulting in a court-created dichotomy of competing public and private rights of use that are subject to constant change as rights are asserted or lost by either group. Curtis argues that the conflict inherent in this division is not serious and that there is probably more dissension among nonriparians asserting incompatible public rights than there is between riparian owners as a group versus the public as a group.[44]

The western states possess certain similarities in that (1) excluding Texas, they were all carved out of the public domain, and (2) they are generally less populous than the eastern states and most have placed more emphasis on the importance of outdoor recreation. Also, the dry climate of much of the region limits the number of navigable streams. Even though there may be numerous access points through extensive federal lands, there is still the feeling that the public is often denied access to use public surface water resources. In most western states, the scarcity of water has given rise to the long-established custom that the limited water supply had to be put to beneficial use, which normally meant off-stream consumptive uses such as irrigation. However, there is some evidence that the institutional structure is gradually changing to reflect the view that in-stream surface water uses such as recreation are also proper beneficial uses.[45]

There appears to be almost complete uniformity among the western states regarding the right of public use on waters where the state owns the streambed. In all the western states except Colorado, the courts have held that the public has a right to use such navigable waters for fishing, commercial travel, recreation, and otherwise. The early cases tended to lump together both the issue of streambed ownership and the right of public use. If the state owned the streambed, then the public had a right of use; if the bed was privately owned, then there was no public right. Usually only the larger streams of the West have been declared navigable. These encompass streams that were meandered or surveyed during the original government surveys of the public domain and include the Missouri and Yellowstone Rivers. Another basis for finding a stream navigable is its ability to support commerce and transportation of goods to market, at least on a seasonal basis, and of course many of the larger western rivers did at one time support such commerce.[46]

Though the right of public use is established on state-owned streams in the West, some states also recognize to varying degrees the public rights to use small streams and lakes where the bed is privately owned. This is based on the common-law notion that society's needs require a public right of use, essentially for recreation. Despite the growing number of cases involving public access to water in western jurisdictions, the number is still quite small compared to cases involving water rights or consumptive water use, and according to Johnson and Austin, "the field is sufficiently new so that most development lies in the future."[47] Rapidly expanding population in most western states and increasing recreational demands seem to assure that public–private rights conflicts involving surface use of water will increase proportionately.

As previously noted, Texas is an exception among western states in that nearly all of its land is privately owned. Texas is also unique in having a long-standing statutory definition of navigability based on the width of the streambed from the mouth upstream. Clear definition of public and private rights is further complicated by the fact that Texas land grants, with their attendant property rights, have emanated from Spain, Mexico, the Republic of Texas, and the state. The right of public access to inland waters, permitted public uses, and the use of beds, banks, and shores remain among the most poorly defined and understood areas of Texas water law.[48] The problems of maintaining minimum in-stream flow and protecting estuarine quality were partially alleviated in comprehensive water legislation enacted in 1985.

Though the federal government has immense power over water resources through such provisions as the commerce clause of the U.S. Constitution, in most cases the full constitutional powers are not exercised, and most water rights and water use problems have been left to the states. However, federal legislation dealing with water quality, protection of endangered species and their habitats, and other environmental issues may indirectly open the way for federal intervention in the protection of in-stream flow and may broadly affect both surface water and groundwater resources. The more specific impact on public use can usually only be inferred rather than addressed directly.

Some scholars are of the opinion that ultimately the common-law "public trust" doctrine may be used to more adequately resolve many in-stream flow and public use problems, and there is heightened interest in the doctrine as a tool for environmental protection. Where the use of streams and estuaries for navigation, commerce, and fisheries is fairly extensive, there seems to be little doubt that the doctrine may be applicable to these uses.[49] Expansion of the original narrow scope of the doctrine means that recreational and aesthetic values may also be legitimate objects of the public trust. Still, use of this doctrine will be less effective in protecting in-stream flow and enhancing public use than specific legislative protection. It can only result in piecemeal protection on a suit-by-suit basis, something much less efficacious than comprehensive legislative protection of these interests.

CHANGING WATER POLICY

The legal and water management literature contains innumerable recommendations for sweeping change of existing water law. These suggestions are usually based on exhaustive analyses of current law and cite appropriate case law and statutory and constitutional provisions to support their arguments. However, political realities in most jurisdictions indicate that comprehensive reforms face formidable obstacles to being realized. This is particularly true where various unregulated private water rights have a long legal history.

Groundwater law in Texas, where the strict common-law rule has prevailed since the turn of the nineteenth century, provides an illustration. The English rule is said to encourage a race for the available groundwater supply and to promote rapid and sometimes wasteful use of the dwindling resource. According to Clawson, such a system "almost forces each landowner to use whatever water he can get before someone else uses it."[50] One study concluded that if imported water were recharged to the nonrenewable Ogallala aquifer of the Texas high plains, it would diffuse to such an extent that landowners who refused to cooperate in financing recharge could pump and use the water injected by others.[51]

Texas courts have generally adopted a hands-off policy in groundwater litigation. Attempts to persuade the courts to alter the common-law rule have been singularly unsuccessful, despite recognition that "some aspects of the common law rule are harsh and outmoded."[52] It has long been argued that the legal basis for this rule, that percolating groundwater is moving in a secret and unknown fashion beneath the surface, is no longer true. There are voluminous data on the extent of major and minor aquifers, the quantity of water in storage, recharge and discharge rates, and rates of depletion; and the performance of some aquifers under various rates of pumpage can be modeled. Still, in one of the few recent significant groundwater cases, *Friendswood Development Co.* v. *Smith-Southwest Industries, Inc.*, the Texas Supreme Court stated: "Providing policy and regulatory procedures in this field is a legislative function. . . . [Our] courts are not equipped to regulate groundwater use and subsidence on a suit-by-suit basis."[53]

The Texas legislature appears little more inclined to bring about significant reform. Of 1985 water legislation, the most comprehensive water law reforms of recent years, Kramer described the groundwater management provisions as "the lengthiest, but perhaps the least meaningful part of the 1985 water package."[54] The political power wielded by the vast number of landowners with private, and largely unregulated, groundwater rights is obvious and constitutes a major obstacle to significant legislative change of the system. The other western states never recognized or long ago replaced the strict common-law rule for groundwater, and only Texas still applies it.

Reform comes easier to those jurisdictions without long histories of unfettered private rights. Even though some states, such as Arizona, have been successful in achieving major reforms, these changes have not come without considerable opposition. Waddle identified the overriding issue as being one of who should have control over water resources, which in turn may make largely academic the question of what could most effectively be done. In Texas there is the general feeling that if groundwater must be regulated, it should be achieved through local agencies, a view strongly shared by West Texas irrigators.[55] The general opposition to control of private individuals' water rights at any level is understandable. For example, few landowners with well-recognized, unregulated water rights of long standing will voluntarily cooperate in a regulatory program. The effects of groundwater depletion are slow to manifest themselves, do not touch all users equally or simultaneously, and may delay remedial action until it is too late.

Recently, models have been developed that aid water resource planners in the formulation of water management policies.[56] The impacts that the various legal and political constraints, such as those mentioned here, have on optimum plans can thus be evaluated. However, prime consideration in such analyses must still be given the constraints imposed by water law. Some legal, political, and social constraints are subject to change in the near future, while others are not, making some desirable alternative solutions unattainable. Despite notions to the contrary, experience seems to indicate that appropriate institutional changes take place very slowly in most jurisdictions. The absolute constraints of water rights law thus can have a limiting effect on the range of possible solutions. Still, such planning studies are useful because proper dissemination of information showing the economic and environmental impacts of unattainable alternatives may eventually serve to convince the public and water users that change of the institutional structure is desirable, if not imperative.

CONCLUSION

This chapter has attempted to show that American geographers have contributed in several ways to the analysis of water law problems in this country and that the law-geography interface involving water law can indeed be a dynamic frontier for both disciplines. Geographers can use their techniques of spatial analysis to examine the impact and constraints of water law institutions on water use, land use, water-based recreation, regional economic development, and so on, and their knowledge of the physical nature of water resources can help lawyers and the courts develop water management institutions better suited to particular environmental conditions and a dwindling water supply. For their part, lawyers can help make geographers involved in water resource management more aware of the often exceedingly complex legal institutions that effectively control water use and water rights allocation. One particular issue should be of concern to both geographers and lawyers: Where possible, water law and water rights should be viewed in the context of a total integrated resource. As scientific knowledge of the nature of water resources and the operation of the hydrologic cycle grows, courts and legislatures should be able to anticipate and avoid prospective conflicts and problems of coordinated water resource use and management such as those discussed here. As human ability to interfere with and control the movement of water in the hydrologic cycle increases, recognition of new, comprehensive private water rights in any phase or the extension of the scope of existing rights should be undertaken only with considerable caution. Duisberg perceptively noted that care must be taken to avoid entangling resources in a maze of legal, political, and private property rights problems from which they cannot be easily extricated for eventual uses of higher value.[57] This advice is especially practical for those concerned with the numerous water law problems and issues for which the applicable law is still unsettled and in the process of development.

NOTES

1. Edward Ackerman, ed. (1965), *The Science of Geography*. National Academy of Sciences, National Research Council, Publication 1277.

2. Derwent Whittlesey (1939), *The Earth and the State*. New York: Henry Holt.

3. For example, see Harlan H. Barrows (1938), "A National Plan and Policy for the Control and Use of Water Resources," in *Geographic Aspects of International Relations,* edited by Charles C. Colby (Chicago: University of Chicago Press); Gilbert F. White (1958), *Human Adjustment to Floods: A Geographical Approach to the Flood Problem in the United States* (Chicago: Department of Geography, University of Chicago); Gilbert F. White (1957), "A Perspective on River Basin Development," *Law and Contemporary Problems,* 22, pp. 157–187; Gilbert F. White (1974), "Role of Geography in Water Resources Management," in *Man and Water,* edited by L. Douglas James (Lexington: University of Kentucky Press).

4. Edward Hamming (1958), "Water Legislation," *Economic Geography,* 34, pp. 42–46.

5. I have addressed all these water law and water rights issues in publications cited in the following sections. In particular, this chapter represents a significant revision and update of Otis W. Templer (1988), "Water Rights Issues," in *The Role of the Social and Behavioral Sciences in Water Resource Management,* edited by Duane D. Baumann and Yacov Y. Haimes (New York: American Society of Civil Engineers).

6. O. Paul Matthews (1984), *Geography and Water Law.* Washington, D.C.: Association of American Geographers.

7. See, for example, O. Paul Matthews (1988), "The Supreme Court, the Commerce Clause and Natural Resources," *Environmental Management,* 12, pp. 413–427; O. Paul Matthews (1994), "Changing the Appropriation Doctrine Under the Model State Water Code," *Water Resources Bulletin,* 30, pp. 189–196; O. Paul Matthews (1994), "Judicial Resolution of Transboundary Water Conflicts," *Water Resources Bulletin,* 30, pp. 375–383; Zachary L. McCormick (1994), "Interstate Water Allocation Compacts in the Western United States — Some Suggestions," *Water Resources Bulletin,* 30, pp. 385–395; Mary McNally (1994), "Water Marketing: The Case of Indian Reserved Rights," *Water Resources Bulletin,* 30, pp. 963–970; James L. Wescoat (1984), *Integrated Water Development: Water Use and Conservation Practice in Western Colorado* (Chicago: Department of Geography, University of Chicago); James L. Wescoat (1985), "On Water Conservation and Reform of the Prior Appropriation Doctrine in Colorado," *Economic*

Geography, 61, pp. 3–24; James L. Wescoat (1986), "Impacts of Federal Salinity Control on Water Rights Allocation Patterns in the Colorado River Basin," *Annals,* Association of American Geographers, 76, pp. 157–174; Fred M. Shelley (1983), "Groundwater Supply Depletion in West Texas: The Farmer's Perspective," *Texas Business Review,* 57, pp. 279–284; Jacque Emel and T. Maddock (1986), "Effectiveness and Equity of Groundwater Management Methods in the Western United States," *Environmental Professional,* 8, pp. 225–236; Jacque Emel and M. Yitayew (1987), "Water Duties: Arizona's Groundwater Management Approach," *Journal of Water Resources Planning and Management,* 113, pp. 82–96; Jacque Emel and Elizabeth Brooks (1988), "Changes in Form and Function of Property Rights Institutions Under Threatened Resource Scarcity," *Annals,* Association of American Geographers, 78, pp. 241–252; Jacque Emel, Rebecca S. Roberts, and David Sauri (1992), "Ideology, Property and Groundwater Resources: An Exploration of Relations," *Political Geography,* 11, pp. 37–54; Rebecca S. Roberts and Sally L. Gros (1987), "The Politics of Ground-Water Management Reform in Oklahoma," *Ground Water,* 25, pp. 535–544; Rebecca S. Roberts (1992), "Groundwater Management Institutions," in *Groundwater Exploitation in the High Plains,* edited by David E. Kromm and Stephen E. White (Lawrence: University of Kansas Press).

8.   L. A. Teclaff (1979), "An International Comparison of Trends in Water Resources Management," *Ecology Law Quarterly,* 7, pp. 881–913.

9.   William Goldfarb (1984), *Water Law.* Boston: Butterworth.

10.   David H. Getches (1984), *Water Law in a Nutshell.* St. Paul: West Publishing Company.

11.   Matthews (1984), op. cit.

12.   Getches (1984), op. cit.

13.   Goldfarb (1984), op. cit.

14.   Getches (1984), op. cit.

15.   Matthews (1984), op. cit.

16.   Goldfarb (1984), op. cit.

17.   Templer (1988), op. cit.

18.   A. M. Piper and H. E. Thomas (1958), "Hydrology and Water Law: What Is Their Common Ground?" in *Water Resources and the Law* (Ann Arbor: University of Michigan School of Law); Otis W. Templer (1973), "Water Law and the Hydrologic Cycle: A Texas Example," *Water Resources Bulletin,* 9, pp. 273–283; Otis W. Templer (1983), "Legal Constraints on Water Resource Management in Texas," *Environmental Professional,* 5, pp. 72–83; Otis W. Templer (1992), "Hydrology and Texas Water Law: A Logician's Nightmare," *Great Plains Research,* 2, pp. 25–48.

19.   William F. Dolson (1966), "Diffused Surface Water and Riparian Rights — Legal Doctrine in Conflict," *Wisconsin Law Review,* pp. 58–120; Templer (1973), op. cit., Matthews (1984), op. cit.

20.   H. E. Thomas (1955), *Water Rights in Areas of Ground-water Mining.* Washington, D.C.: United States Geological Survey.

21. H. E. Thomas (1951), *The Conservation of Groundwater.* New York: McGraw-Hill.

22. Dolson (1966), op. cit.

23. Templer (1973), op. cit.

24. Otis W. Templer (1981), "Weather Modification: A Controversial Issue on the Texas High Plains," *Journal of Arid Environments,* 4, pp. 71–84.

25. *Southwest Weather Research, Inc.* v. *Duncan,* 319 S.W.2d 940, Tex. Civ. App. (1958).

26. Wells A. Hutchins, *The Texas Law of Water Rights* (Austin: Texas Board of Water Engineers, 1961); Victor Bouldin (1955), "Rights in Diffused Surface Water in Texas," *Proceedings,* Water Law Conference, University of Texas School of Law. Also see Otis W. Templer (1978), "An Analysis of Playa Lake Water Utilization on the Texas High Plains," *Water Resources Bulletin,* 14, pp. 454–465; Otis W. Templer (1982), "Irrigation and Playa Lakes on the Texas High Plains," *Texas Business Review,* 56, pp. 169–174.

27. Wells A. Hutchins (1971), *Water Rights Laws in the Nineteen Western States* (Washington, D.C.: United States Department of Agriculture, Economic Research Service, Natural Resources Economics Division); Matthews (1984), op. cit.; Paul M. Ginsburg (1968), "Ownership of Diffused Surface Water in the West," *Stanford Law Review,* 20, pp. 1205–1229.

28. Frank J. Trelease (1954), "Coordination of Riparian and Appropriative Rights to the Use of Water," *Texas Law Review,* 33, pp. 24–69.

29. Doug Caroom and Paul Elliott (1981), "Water Rights Adjudication — Texas Style," *Texas Bar Journal,* 44, pp. 1183–1190; Otis W. Templer (1973), "Institutional Constraints and Water Resources: Water Rights Adjudication in Texas," *Rocky Mountain Social Science Journal,* 10, pp. 37–45; Otis W. Templer (1985), "Water Resource Management, Water Rights Adjudication and the Stacy Reservoir Decision: No Place but Texas," *Papers and Proceedings,* Applied Geography Conference, 8, pp. 63–68.

30. Otis W. Templer (1978), "Texas Groundwater Law: Inflexible Institutions and Resource Realities," *Ecumene,* 10, pp. 6–15; Otis W. Templer (1987), "The 1985 Water Legislation and Groundwater Management in Texas," *Forum,* Association for Arid Lands Studies, 3, pp. 3–10; Otis W. Templer (1989), "Adjusting to Groundwater Depletion: The Case of Texas and Lessons for the Future of the Southwest," in *Water and the Future of the Southwest,* edited by Zachary A. Smith (Albuquerque: University of New Mexico Press).

31. *Houston and Texas Central Railway Company* v. *East,* 98 Tex. 1416; 81 S.W. 279, Texas Sup.Ct. (1904).

32. Otis W. Templer (1980), "Conjunctive Management of Water Resources in the Context of Texas Water Law," *Water Resources Bulletin,* 16, pp. 305–311.

33. Thomas (1951), op. cit.

34. Templer (1980), op. cit.

35. W. A. Hutchins (1958), "Ground Water Legislation," *Rocky Mountain Law Review,* 30, pp. 416–440.

36. Hutchins (1958), op. cit. However, see Otis W. Templer and James E. Jonish (1994), "Managing Texas' Unique Edwards Aquifer: A Critique," *Forum,* Association for Arid Lands Studies, 9, pp. 57–64. In the Edwards aquifer region near San Antonio, ground- and surface water are closely interconnected. Federal or state authorities threaten to impose conjunctive water management to protect "critical habitats" in this environmentally sensitive area. Even so, more stringent control of groundwater rights would probably apply to this one unique situation and not to a broader region or the whole state.

37. R. E. Clark, ed. (1967), *Water and Water Rights.* Indianapolis: Allen Smith Co.

38. Otis W. Templer (1986), "Protecting Instream Flow and Estuarine Quality: Continuing Legal Problems in Texas," *Papers and Proceedings,* Applied Geography Conference, 9, pp. 63–72; Goldfarb (1984), op. cit.; J. M. Bagley, Dean T. Larsen, and Lee Kapalski (1985), "Satisfying Instream Flow Needs Under Western Water Rights," *Journal of Water Resources Planning and Management,* 111, pp. 171–191; W. D. Dixon and W. E. Cox (1985), "Minimum Flow Protection in Riparian States," *Journal of Water Resources Planning and Management,* 111, pp. 149–156; Corwin W. Johnson (1973), "Legal Assurances of Adequate Flows of Fresh Water Into Texas' Bays and Estuaries to Maintain Proper Salinity Levels," *Houston Law Review,* 10, pp. 598–640.

39. Raymond L. Anderson (1982), "Conflict Between Establishment of Instream Flows and Other Water Uses in the Western States," *Water Resources Bulletin,* 18, pp. 61–66.

40. A. W. Stone, "Public Rights in Water Uses and Private Rights in Land Adjacent to Water," in Clark (1967), op. cit.

41. Stone (1967), op. cit.

42. National Water Commission (1973), *Water Policies for the Future.* Port Washington, N.Y.: Water Information Center.

43. Ralph W. Johnson and Russell A. Austin Jr. (1967), "Recreational Rights and Titles to Beds on Western Lakes and Streams," *Natural Resources Journal,* 7, pp. 1–52.

44. E. J. Curtis (1977), "Some Legal Aspects of River Recreation Management in the East," in *River Recreation Management and Research.* St. Paul, Minnesota: USDA Forest Service, North Central Forest Experiment Station, General Technical Report NC-28.

45. Johnson and Austin (1967), op. cit.

46. Johnson and Austin (1967), op. cit.

47. Johnson and Austin (1967), op. cit.

48. Otis W. Templer (1979), "Problems of Public Access to Water in Texas Lakes and Streams: An Analysis" Texas Tech University, Lubbock, Water Resources Center, Report WRC-79-1.

49. E. S. Casey (1984), "Water Law — Public Trust Doctrine," *Natural Resources Journal,* 24, pp. 809–825; M. E. Morrison and M. K. Dollahite (1985), "The Public Trust Doctrine: Insuring Needs of Texas Bays and Estuaries," *Baylor Law Review,* 37,

pp. 365–424; J. L. Weaver (1985), "The Public Trust Doctrine and Texas Water Rights Administration: Common Law Protection for Texas Bays and Estuaries," *State Bar of Texas Environmental Law Journal,* 15, pp. 1–10.

50. Marion Clawson (1963), "Critical Review of Man's History in Arid Regions," in *Aridity and Man,* edited by Carl Hodge and Peter C. Duisberg. Washington, D.C.: American Association for the Advancement of Science.

51. Michael J. Mocek, B. J. Claborne, and Dan M. Wells (1971), "Conjunctive Use of Water in West Texas — Benefits to Non-Cooperators," Texas Tech University, Water Resources Center, Report WRC-71-6.

52. Corwin W. Johnson (1982), "Reform of Texas Groundwater Law," in *Proceedings,* 1982 Water for Texas Conference, Water Issues for Today, for Tomorrow; Corwin W. Johnson (1982), "Texas Groundwater Law: A Survey and Some Proposals," *Natural Resources Journal,* 22, pp. 1017–1030; Corwin W. Johnson (1986), "The Continuing Voids in Texas Groundwater Law: Are Concepts and Terminology to Blame?" *St. Mary's Law Journal,* 17, pp. 1281–1295.

53. *Friendswood Development Company* v. *Smith-Southwest Industries, Inc.,* 576 S.W.2d. 21, Texas Sup.Ct. (1978).

54. Kenneth W. Kramer (1985/86), "The Texas Water Package: The Beginning of a New Era or Business as Usual?" *State Bar of Texas Environmental Law Journal,* 16, pp. 57–63.

55. Don Graf (1982), "The Case for Local Regulation," *Cross Section,* 28, pp. 1–4; Shelley (1983), op. cit.

56. J. J. Doody (1969), "Conjunctive Use of Ground and Surface Waters," *Journal of the American Water Works Association,* 61, pp. 395–397; M. L. Livingston (1985), "Treating Water Institutions as Endogenous Variables: Demonstration of a Conceptual Model," *Water Resources Bulletin,* 21, pp. 23–29.

57. Peter Duisberg, "Challenge of the Future," in Hodge and Duisberg (1963), op. cit.

5

THE GEOGRAPHICAL BASIS OF LAND USE LAW

RUTHERFORD H. PLATT

Collaboration between the disciplines of geography and law is unusual but inevitable. The two fields are natural allies in the planning and management of land and water resources. This chapter addresses the land side of this relationship, specifically, the geographical basis for judicial decisions resolving land use disputes. My thesis is that judicial perception of geographical factors underlies many, if not most, legal decisions involving land use. In particular, the problem of the "taking issue," which lies at the heart of constitutional review of land use controls, is inherently based on geographical factors.

Like Molière's character in *Le Bourgeois Gentilhomme* who learned he had been talking prose all his life without realizing it, land use lawyers have long "practiced geography," at least crudely, without necessarily recognizing the fact. The corollary of this assertion is that the more geographical analysis is explicitly introduced into the legal process (including legislation, administrative rules, and adjudication), the fairer and more effective will be the results for society.

In this chapter I attempt to address each of these constituencies to the extent possible within the scope of one chapter. The first section reviews some pertinent concepts of geography for the benefit of nongeographers, and a later section summarizes the legal process for the nonlawyer. I then turn to the role of geographical context — or, more precisely, the judicial perception of that context — as a basis for the outcome of a series of land use decisions.

GEOGRAPHICAL PERSPECTIVES ON LAND USE

The field of geography is inherently eclectic. Its two major branches, physical and human geography, are in turn divided into a number of subfields that respectively contribute to an understanding of the nature and use of land resources. On the physical side, these subfields include geomorphology, hydrology, biogeography, and climatology; on the human side, urban, political, economic, cultural, and social geography, among other specialties. Some geographical topics bridge the physical-human dichotomy, as in studies of human response to natural hazards.

It has sometimes been charged that geographers have more in common with their colleagues in cognate disciplines than they do with one another. There are, however, certain organizing themes that characterize the geographic perspective and method as distinct from other disciplines. These include the concepts of spatial organization, scale, function, and externalities.

Spatial Organization

A common denominator that unites geographers of all specialties is a fundamental concern with the organization or distribution of diverse phenomena in space. Spatiality is to geography what spirituality is to the ministry and health is to the physician. The identification and explanation of areal differentiation of diverse phenomena, notably including land use, is a long-standing geographical pursuit.

Geographers are concerned with the where and the why of spatial patterns on the earth's surface. To delineate the where, geographers utilize maps, photographs, graphs, and other means of representing spatial data. Cartography, the development and preparation of maps suitable for particular tasks, is itself a subfield of geography. To explain spatial patterns requires the application of various sources of inference, including statistical analysis, empirical field research, modeling, and scholarly intuition. Geographical analysis often involves the identification of cross-relationships between different systems of spatial data.

Spatial differentiation of land use may be interpreted in terms of the interaction of three overlapping categories, or "macrosystems," of spatial data: (1) physical phenomena, (2) human socioeconomic activities (referred to by geographers as "cultural phenomena"), and (3) units of legal and political authority over land. The physical landscape may be described and interpreted in terms of the spatial characteristics of bedrock and landforms, soils, hydrology, natural vegetation, wildlife, and climate. Each of these subclasses of physical data represents a major branch of natural science. The geographer draws upon the findings of the appropriate field to the level of detail necessary to resolve the problem under consideration.

The geography of "cultural" human activity patterns includes systems of rural land use — agriculture, forestry, and mining — as well as urban settlements ranging from hamlets to metropolitan regions. Aggregate human activity patterns reflect systems of economic enterprise. It has been argued that human geography is basically economic geography. The spatial analysis of economic systems involves the identification of "nodes," or points of activity, and "linkages," or connections between nodes such as transportation corridors, pipelines, and communications networks. Such linkages expedite the flow of people, goods, information, and capital between places.

Spatial patterns of legal and political authority may be analogized to a series of jurisdictional templates overlying land that represent (1) ownership (private or public); (2) minor civil divisions (municipalities, special districts, counties); (3) states; and (4) the federal government. Units of authority at each level are bounded by precise if irregular territorial limits that define the geographic reach of their legal power over land. Moreover, units at different levels in the hierarchy influence the use of land within their jurisdictions in different ways according to their respective legal, political, and fiscal capabilities. The use of individual parcels of land thus reflects a complex interaction among the various levels of land managers that share jurisdiction over a given site. Broader patterns of land use result from the aggregation of use characteristics of individual parcels.

Legal and political boundaries are of course invisible to observation unless marked by a sign, fence, or other visual indicator. But the presence of institutional boundaries may often be inferred from observation of abrupt changes in land use patterns, as from a high-income, low-density residential district to an adjoining area of congestion, commerce, clutter, and blight. The fortuitous location of legal and political boundaries often exerts substantial influence upon the arrangement of human activities and perceived land use patterns. Of course, institutional patterns are not totally independent variables. Particularly in the case of suburban jurisdictions established in this century, political boundaries tend to both reflect and in turn reinforce the spatial arrangement of housing markets, economic activity, and locational preferences of the wealthy.[1]

Scale

Fundamental to geographic analysis of spatial organization is the concept of scale, or hierarchy. Certain kinds of spatial variability may be classified according to position within a hierarchy of "nested subsets" of phenomena that comprise the overall spatial system under consideration. In the physical context, for instance, a riparian system may be divided into a hierarchy of mainstream, major tributaries, subtributaries, and headwaters, each with its associated area of surface drainage or watershed. For purposes of land planning and water management — both important legal concerns — the position of a tract of land in relation to this hierarchy of drainage is crucial.

Patterns of economic activity and human settlement are also hierarchical. Commercial centers may be classified in terms of size and complexity, from a small village to a major metropolitan area. The position of a particular settlement in this hierarchy is not accidental. Geographers have developed numerous theories and models to account for the spatial organization of urban systems. Central-place theory relates the size and spacing of commercial centers to the distance consumers are willing to travel to obtain certain goods and services. Thus beer, bread, and milk are purchased from the nearest among a myriad of neighborhood or "convenience" outlets. New cars, banking, legal, and health services are obtained from larger ("higher order") centers. Rare art objects, fur coats, large-scale financing, and expensive luxury automobiles are likely to be available only in a major metropolitan city. Commercial centers at each higher level thus provide a wider array of goods and services to consumers from a broader geographic "hinterland." Concomitantly, the size and diversity of a commercial center is limited by its proximity to competing centers of the same or higher order.[2]

The location of a tract of land in relation to the hierarchy of urban places, like its position in a drainage system, bears an important relationship to its economic value for particular uses. The history of American land settlement is replete with examples of speculative land ventures that failed to achieve the shining prosperity predicted by their promoters in part because of locational disadvantages. For every Chicago or St. Louis, there has been many a disappointed Michigan City (Indiana) or Cairo (Illinois). The equivalent in contemporary metropolitan America is the proliferation of municipal zoning for regional shopping centers and office parks, regardless of the need or potential viability of such uses in a particular location.

Function

A closely related notion to that of hierarchy is the concept of function. The raison d'être of a human settlement and its size and level in the central-place hierarchy are determined by the function(s) it performs. An urban place without a function is a virtual nullity, regardless of what laws or promoters may say.

The colonial legislatures of Virginia and Maryland attempted to encourage the growth of towns by laying out sites adjoining rivers and granting them special port privileges. The region, however, shipped its products directly from river landings at each plantation and needed no port towns. In the pithy words of Thomas Jefferson (a geographer, among his other vocations), "The laws have said there shall be towns; but nature has said there shall not, and they remain unworthy of enumeration."[3]

Urban economic functions may take the form of primary (agriculture, forestry, mining), secondary (manufacturing), or tertiary (retail and service) activities or a combination of them. Urban functions change over time with technological innovation, patterns of economic investment (both intra- and international), demographic and lifestyle trends, shifts in political power, and changing popular perception. Thus urban places may lose or gain in their range of functions and correspondingly in their size and importance within the national system of settlements.

The notion of function also may be applied to individual parcels of land or real property. This concept relates each discrete unit of land to the larger physical and human spatial systems of which it is a component. In ecological terms, land in its natural state may facilitate recharge of groundwater, store surface runoff in soil moisture or ponding, support vegetation, concentrate energy through photosynthesis, and provide habitat for wildlife. Land within the agricultural system functions as cropland, pasture, fallow, horticulture, or farmstead. Urban land functions as a site for residential, commercial, industrial, institutional, or recreational activities.

The notion of function is related to but not synonymous with land use. Function refers to the relationship between a parcel of land and the wider physical and socioeconomic spatial systems to which it belongs. Even vacant land that is "unused" in a market sense may function in a physical and socioeconomic sense, and such functions may be either positive or negative to the surrounding area. Thus a vacant urban lot may have no formal "use" but may function as visual amenity, perceptual buffer between urban activities, play space for children, habitat for wildlife, and, negatively, as a dumping site for trash and hazardous wastes or a refuge for the homeless.

Externalities

The concept of function suggests that no parcel of land is an "island" unto itself. The use or condition of any unit of land generates external effects, or "externalities," upon surrounding areas. Such effects, which may be either positive or negative, result from the inconsistency of the various patterns of spatial organization of land — physical, socioeconomic, and institutional. While the authority of land managers is confined to the geographic space defined by their jurisdictional boundaries, the physical and socioeconomic consequences of their actions are distributed according to the spatial pattern of the variable considered.

Externalities arise between units of land management at each level of legal and political authority — ownership, municipality, county, state, national. Since land managers are primarily concerned with the *internal* benefits and costs (i.e., effects arising within their own territories), they tend to ignore externalities arising from their land use policies or actions. While the nature, extent, and economic consequences of externalities vary according to the scale at which they arise, the fundamental problem is the same: How can favorable externalities be encouraged and adverse externalities suppressed or mitigated? The geographer, having thus framed the problem, refers its solution to the law.

LEGAL PERSPECTIVES ON LAND USE

The landscape of the lawyer is very different from that of the geographer. While the latter is a composite of several interacting types of spatial phenomena — physical, economic, social, and institutional — the law is primarily concerned with the last category — legal and political authority over land — and only secondarily with the others. Where the geographer's model of the economy identifies systems of nodes, linkages, flows, hierarchies, and functions, the lawyer's view might be better described as a battlefield on which private property interests struggle against each other as well as against governmental constraints imposed on behalf of the "public interest." This landscape is crisscrossed with earthworks of entrenched legal interests and littered with the shell craters of past legal salvos.

The adversarial perspective of law contrasts with the deterministic orientation of geography. Land use patterns to the lawyer are the collective outcome of a myriad of individual cases, conflicts, appeals, administrative rulings, and political actions to which geographical notions of scale, function, and central-place theory may seem irrelevant abstractions. The holistic, systematic perspective of geography yields to the particularistic, adjudicative focus of the law. Within the law substantive outcomes — particularly broad-scale, long-term implications — are secondary to constitutional issues of fairness and reasonableness of the process by which such conflicting interests are resolved.

The recognition of competing interests is itself an important difference between geography and law. The former identifies spatially differentiated "clusters" of common interest defined by diverse criteria. In contrast to this fluid and dynamic approach, the law rigidly confines its recognition of legitimate "parties in interest" in land use controversies to those deemed to possess legal "standing" that qualifies them to seek legal redress. Classes of parties with legal standing in land use disputes normally are limited to property owners directly affected by a decision, their immediate neighbors, the municipality, the state, and the federal government. Other geographically relevant constituencies such as the neighborhood, downstream watershed occupants, or the metropolitan region lack legal standing except to the extent that an organizational surrogate may successfully claim to represent affected interests.

The complex "nested hierarchies" of political geography are collapsed into a single monolithic "public" in the eyes of the law. This blurs or erases geographical distinctions between diverse "publics" with very different interests — neighborhood, community, region, state, nation, globe.

With all the contrasts indicated above, can it be said that geography and law occupy any common ground? The answer is strongly affirmative. It was suggested above that the problem of externalities is a point of overlap between the geographical and legal frames of reference. Externalities, which represent friction among components in the geographer's macroview of the land economy, are in fact the central concern of the lawyer's microview. If there were no externalities among land use management units, there would be no need for land use law.

Both the private (owner v. owner) and the public (owner v. "public") branches of land use law are fundamentally concerned with the problem of externalities. And this problem is fundamentally geographical.

THE LEGAL PROCESS

Before exploring the foregoing proposition, the nonlegal reader must understand the context in which the law of land use is articulated. The starting point is the U.S. Constitution — the "supreme law of the land." The Constitution and its state counterparts establish fundamental principles governing the relationship between government (federal, state, municipal) on the one hand and the private individual on the other. Of particular importance to the land use context is the Fifth Amendment, which declares: "No person shall be . . . deprived of life, liberty, or property without due process of law, nor shall private property be taken for public use without just compensation."

Responsibility for the establishment of laws concerning land use lies with the individual states, which in turn have delegated most of their authority to local municipalities. Pursuant to state enabling laws, local municipalities (and counties for many unincorporated areas) may adopt land use zoning laws and other measures regulating private use of land. In recent years many states have adopted additional laws establishing statewide regulations for particular types of sensitive or significant areas such as floodplains, wetlands, historic sites, and agricultural land.[4] State and municipal laws may further delegate authority to administrative bodies to promulgate specific rules that elaborate upon the broader provisions of the statute.

Statutes and administrative regulations concerning land use are subject to judicial review upon suit by an "aggrieved party" against the public entity whose action is in question. The court is asked to resolve whether the measure is constitutional and fairly applied to the plaintiff. Many suits are decided on procedural grounds without reaching the merits of the case. Others are found to be "fairly debatable" on their merits, and the legislative action is presumed to be valid. In a third set of decisions, courts are persuaded by the plaintiff that the public measure is "discriminatory, arbitrary, or capricious," and the measure is held invalid, at least as applied to the plaintiff. The latter two classes of decisions thus involve some degree of judicial scrutiny of the facts of the case, including its geographic context.

The unsuccessful party in the trial court may appeal the case to a higher court, which may affirm or reverse the decision below. Occasionally, cases are appealed as far as the Supreme Court, which decided about twenty major land use cases during the 1970s and 1980s.

Published decisions on land use cases in the state and federal court systems comprise a rich archive of judicial perspectives on the relationship of law and geography. It is the role of the attorneys for each party to portray applicable legal authority and the facts of the case favorably to their respective positions. The court in turn forms its own opinion of the state of the law and the facts of the case and reaches a decision accordingly. The legal outcome therefore reflects the court's perception of the geographic context.

Judges, being human, do not necessarily view the circumstances of a land use issue in the same way. Disagreement may arise between individual judges on a multijudge court, between a lower and a higher court reviewing the same case, between courts in different states or federal jurisdictions reviewing similar cases, and between courts considering similar issues at different points in time.

The last category is particularly important in weighing the role of geographical perspective in the judicial process. Law is a flexible and dynamic institution. The adjudicative process permits reinterpretation of legal principles over time in response to actual or perceived changes in society and its needs. As stated by the U.S. Supreme Court in *Village of Euclid* v. *Ambler Realty Co.,* "While the meaning of the constitutional guarantees never varies, the scope of their application must expand or contract to meet the new and different conditions which are constantly coming within the field of their operation."[5] Leading decisions on similar land use issues over time may thus reflect shifts of legal response to "new and different conditions," among which geographical conditions loom large.

GEOGRAPHICAL FACTORS IN LAND USE DECISIONS

With this background, we can now review some actual judicial decisions to examine more closely the role of judicial perception of geographical factors, as reflected in the legal outcome. Each of the contexts of potential judicial disagreement listed above is represented among the cases reviewed. We consider cases drawn from the private law of nuisance along with the public law of land use control.

Nuisance: "Balancing the Equities"

The law of nuisance is derived from the English common law, which dates back to the early Middle Ages. Nuisance is concerned with mitigating harms inflicted by users of property upon their neighbors or upon the general public. Offensive conduct affecting surrounding land might include dumping of refuse, causing the flooding of adjacent land, or polluting the air or water. A monetary penalty levied against the defendant by the court was often deemed insufficient to redress a continuing economic or health threat to surrounding areas. To remedy such ongoing harms, a plaintiff sought "specific relief" in the form of an injunction or order of the court to the defendant to cease or modify the conduct complained of.

The general principle underlying such law is the doctrine of "balancing the equities." This doctrine involves the court's weighing the economic burden upon the defendant of granting an injunction in comparison with the economic or other harms inflicted on the plaintiffs if the injunction is denied. This exercise is inherently geographic in nature, with the spatial impact of each outcome translated into largely economic terms.

The application of "balancing the equities" in response to different judicial perceptions of the geographic context is illustrated in two contrasting cases involving pollution from cement plants, one from California in 1911 and the other from New York state in 1970. *Hulbert v. California Cement Company*[6] involved a conflict between a cement manufacturing facility and surrounding residential dwellings. The case is typical of private nuisance actions where no public regulations are involved. The court gives detailed attention to the geographic context and chronology of land use change in the vicinity as a guide to its ultimate decision.

The site in question was located at Slover Mountain, near the city of Colton in San Bernardino County. This mountain had long been used as a source of marble and limestone, and lime kilns had been established there for many years before the dispute arose. Orange groves were first introduced to the area after the kilns were in place but before the cement plant was constructed. Other orange groves were planted in the neighborhood after the cement plant began operation. The court noted that these lands were subject to "a well nigh continuous shower of cement dust, emanating from defendant's cement mills and caused by their operation," which formed "an opaque semi-cemented incrustation upon the upper sides of all exposed flowers and foliage, particularly leaves of citrus trees."[7]

The court found that the plaintiffs were suffering ongoing economic harm and personal discomfort from the activities of the defendant. Temporal considerations are very important in nuisance actions. In *Hulbert*, for example, did the plaintiff "come to the nuisance" by moving to the area and planting orange groves after the cement plant was in operation? The court found that some land north of the cement plant had been planted in citrus a year before the cement plant was begun. In weighing the equities, the court acknowledged that the cement plant "is a very important enterprise; that its location is peculiarly adapted for the manufacture of cement; and that great loss may result to the corporation by enforcement of the injunction."[8]

Nevertheless, the court found continuing economic and personal harm suffered by the plaintiffs resulting from this particular plant. The court issued an injunction to curtail the level of cement production, stating: "The right of a man to use and enjoy his property is as supreme as his neighbor's and no artificial use of it by either can be permitted to destroy that of the other." The court held that no feasible technical means existed to abate the smoke pollution and that an award of monetary damages to the plaintiffs would mean "in effect, allowing the seizure of private property for use other than a public one — something unheard of and totally unauthorized in the law."[9]

The *Hulbert* court thus viewed the issue in very narrow geographic terms, limited to the cement plant and its immediate neighbors. It did not consider the larger regional implications of its decision for either the building or citrus fruit industries and the future growth of southern California. The decision adjudicated the rights of the immediate parties and held that a balancing of the equities favored the plaintiffs.

A contrasting result was reached under a different mode of analysis in the New York case of *Boomer* v. *Atlantic Cement Company*.[10] Once again, a group of property owners were suing the operator of a large cement plant, although no damage to agriculture was alleged. The trial court had found that a nuisance was proven and awarded monetary damages to the plaintiffs but not an injunction. The New York Court of Appeals (the state's supreme court) upheld the decision on the grounds that while plaintiffs were indeed harmed severely and were entitled to a monetary payment, nevertheless an injunction was inappropriate. The court noted that the cement plant was one of many in the Hudson River valley and that the problem of cement plant emissions was widespread and defied technical solution: "It seems apparent that the amelioration of air pollution would depend on technical research in great depth. . . . It is likely to involve massive public expenditure and to demand more than any local community can accomplish and to depend on regional and interstate control."[11] Viewing the issue not within the narrow context of the immediate parties, as in *Hulbert*, but as a regional and national policy problem, the court declined to "use a decision in private litigation as a purposeful mechanism to achieve direct public objectives greatly beyond the rights and interests before the court."

In both *Hulbert* and *Boomer*, the plaintiffs succeeded in proving that they were victims of a nuisance or harmful externality from cement plants. The decisions differ in outcome, however, with an injunction granted in *Hulbert* but denied in *Boomer*. This difference in outcome may be ascribed to various factors, including a different court, state, and time period and the advent of state and federal air pollution programs by 1970 to which the *Boomer* court deferred. But an implicit contrast between the decisions is the geographic context and scale in which the court chose to view the issue and the implications of its decision.

Police Power: The "Taking Issue"

The police power is the inherent power of government to regulate private activities, including the use of land, in the interest of the public health, safety, and welfare. Exercise of the police power is noncompensatory, that is, affected private parties are not remunerated for any economic detriment that a public regulation may inflict. Since the advent of modern land use laws in the United States in the early twentieth century, the "taking issue" has been a perennial constraint upon the exercise of the police power. The taking issue involves the extent to which a public police power regulation may reduce private property values before it amounts to a taking of private property "for public use without just compensation," in violation of the Fifth Amendment of the U.S. Constitution.

The taking issue was first articulated in the 1922 U.S. Supreme Court opinion by Justice Oliver Wendell Holmes in *Pennsylvania Coal Co. v. Mahon.*[12] Prior to this decision, as far back as the Magna Carta, "taking for public use" was considered to mean actual and literal use by the public, not merely reduction of value. Mahon irrevocably altered American constitutional law on this point by asserting the possibility that a "taking" might result from regulation alone.

Writing for the majority, Holmes admitted that reduction of economic value is not per se unconstitutional: "Government could hardly go on if, to some extent, values incident to property could not be diminished without paying for every such change."[13] But Holmes declared that "the general rule at least is that property may be regulated to a certain extent. If regulation goes too far, it will be recognized as a taking."[14]

The notion that a regulation may go "too far" introduced into the public law of land use regulation a concept analogous to that of "balancing the equities" in the private law of nuisance. Courts are constantly compelled to weigh the public benefit of a measure against its economic impact on a private owner. However, the factual circumstances of the *Mahon* case (discussed below) that gave rise to Holmes's famous rule were viewed quite differently in a dissenting opinion by Justice Louis Brandeis. *Mahon* involved the constitutionality of a Pennsylvania statute that prohibited mining that could cause subsidence near houses and other buildings. The company asserted a contractual right to excavate coal regardless of subsidence hazards under deeds of mineral rights granted by the surface owners years earlier. In such deeds the surface owners had waived any liability on the part of the coal company for causing damage to houses and other structures. The coal company challenged the statute as an unconstitutional infringement of its private contractual rights and a "taking" of the value of the coal that the statute required to be left in the ground to support the surface.

Despite evidence that the statute was intended to remedy a widespread public hazard, Holmes chose to view the issue narrowly. He wrote:

> This is the case of a single private house. . . . Usually in ordinary private affairs the public interest does not warrant much of this kind of interference. A source of damage to such a house is not a public nuisance, even if similar damage is inflicted on others in different places. The damage is not common or public. On the other hand, the extent of the taking is great. . . . To make it commercially impracticable to mine certain coal has very nearly the same effect for constitutional purposes as appropriating or destroying it.[15]

Holmes recognized that the statute also sought to protect not only private homes but public streets and facilities. He acknowledged that such protection was a desirable public goal but one that should be attained through compensation rather than regulation:

> A strong public desire to improve the public condition is not enough
> to warrant achieving the desire by a shorter cut than the constitu-
> tional way of paying for the change. . . . So far as private persons or
> communities have seen fit to take the risk of acquiring only surface
> rights, we cannot see that the fact that their risk has become a danger
> warrants the giving to them greater rights than they bought.[16]

Like the *Hulbert* court, Holmes focused upon the immediate physical and
legal relationship of the corporate entity on the one hand and the affected property owner on the other. But unlike *Hulbert,* the property owner here was
found to have contractually waived any claim to protection against harm from
the corporate activity. The statute in question was considered to impair the coal
company's property interest in the coal and to serve no substantial *public* interest,
as distinct from the *private* interests of the individual property owners.

Justice Brandeis vigorously disputed Holmes's perception of the geographic
scope of the problem:

> Every restriction upon the use of property, imposed in the exercise of
> the police power, deprives the owner of some right theretofore
> enjoyed, and is, in that sense, an abridgement by the state of rights in
> property without making compensation. But restriction imposed to
> protect the public health, safety, or morals from dangers threatened is
> not a taking. The restriction here in question is merely the prohibi-
> tion of a noxious use. . . . The restriction upon the use of his property
> cannot, of course, be lawfully imposed, unless its purpose is to protect
> the public. But the purpose of a restriction does not cease to be pub-
> lic because incidentally some private persons may thereby receive gra-
> tuitously valuable special benefits.[17]

Thus Brandeis and Holmes parted company on the spatial frame of reference.
Should the benefits of the act be considered largely private and only incidentally
public, or the reverse?

Sixty-five years later, Brandeis would be vindicated. In *Keystone Bituminous
Coal Association v. DeBenedictis,*[18] the U.S. Supreme Court addressed the constitutionality of another Pennsylvania statute adopted in 1966 that prohibited
"coal mining that causes subsidence damage to pre-existing public buildings,
dwellings, and cemeteries." Despite the similarity of the statute to the one
invalidated in *Mahon,* the Supreme Court upheld its constitutionality in a five-
to-four decision. Technically, *Keystone* did not overrule *Mahon* but instead distinguished it on its facts. Unlike Holmes, who viewed the issue in terms of "a
single private house," the majority in *Keystone* emphasized the broad public
issues addressed by the Pennsylvania statute:

> The [1966] Subsidence Act differs from the [1922] Kohler Act in
> critical and dispositive respects. With regard to the Kohler Act, the

court believed that the Commonwealth had acted only to insure against damage to some private land owners' homes. Justice Holmes stated that if the private individuals needed support for their structures, they should not have taken the risk of acquiring only surface rights. . . . Here, by contrast, the Commonwealth is acting to protect the public interest in health, the environment, and the fiscal integrity of the areas.[19]

Keystone reflects a broader judicial recognition of physical and economic externalities created by underground coal mining:

Coal mine subsidence is the lowering of strata overlying a coal mine, including the land surface, caused by the extraction of underground coal. This lowering of the strata can have devastating effects. It often causes substantial damage to foundations, walls, other structural members, and the integrity of houses and buildings. Subsidence frequently causes sink holes or troughs in land, which makes the land difficult or impossible to develop. Its effect on farming has been well documented — many subsided areas cannot be plowed or properly prepared. Subsidence can also cause the loss of groundwater and surface ponds. In short, it presents the type of environmental concern that has been the focus of so much federal, state, and local regulation in recent decades.[20]

In support of these statements, the Court extensively cited scholarly works and government reports on environmental problems of coal mining. In upholding the state law, it affirmed that environmental protection is a proper legislative function (a point also made in *Boomer*).

Keystone thus expanded the scope and sophistication of judicial appraisal of geographic circumstances in comparison with *Mahon*. Yet the majority in *Keystone* discredited the plaintiff's claim of economic harm resulting from the statute. Unlike *Mahon* and a dissent in *Keystone* itself, the majority held that the statute deprived the coal mining industry of only 2 percent more coal than what they would otherwise have to leave in place to protect their own employees from mine collapse.

Keystone did not question Holmes's basic test that "if regulation goes too far, it will be recognized as a taking." But the majority in *Keystone* declined to view the 1966 Subsidence Act as "going too far." Reflecting the evolutionary nature of judicial lawmaking, they stated: "The Subsidence Act is a prime example that 'circumstances may so change in time . . . as to clothe with such a [public] interest what in other times . . . would be a matter of purely private concern.'"[21]

Zoning: "Public Health, Safety, and Welfare"

The advent of comprehensive municipal land use zoning in the United States occurred in New York City in 1916. The New York law was advocated by progressive reformers and real estate interests concerned respectively with urban congestion and neighborhood change.[22] The zoning law divided the city into districts and zones within which different rules were specified for the permissible use of land and the density and bulk of structures to be built upon it. Existing structures and uses were permitted to continue but new development was required to conform to the zoning regulations. This legal innovation of zoning rapidly diffused across the country. By the end of 1925, 420 municipalities with a combined population of 27 million had adopted zoning laws.[23]

Zoning represented a drastic departure from the case-by-case approach to nuisance abatement as represented in the 1911 *Hulbert* case. It also marked a major transition from public laws that addressed a specific nuisance-type activity such as the one involved in *Mahon*. Zoning involved the segregation by district of different types of land used. It exalted the "single-family residence district" from which all other activities were barred. It prescribed permissible uses of vacant land long before any actual development proposal had been made. And as with any exercise of police power, it provided no compensation to adversely affected property owners and thus posed the taking issue, among other constitutional questions.

The constitutionality of zoning was ultimately confirmed by the U.S. Supreme Court in its landmark decision in *Village of Euclid* v. *Ambler Realty Co.*[24] The high court's decision in Euclid was not easily reached, however, and its history reveals much about the role of geographic perception in the judicial process. The immediate dispute that gave rise to the Euclid decision involved a 68-acre tract of undeveloped land situated between a railroad and a highway in the village of Euclid, a suburb of Cleveland, Ohio. Euclid had zoned the plaintiff's highway frontage to a depth of 620 feet for residential purposes only. The balance of the property was largely unrestricted. The lawsuit challenged the constitutionality of zoning per se.

The case was first heard in the federal district court. (A party asserting a federal constitutional ground may choose to file suit in the federal courts rather than the state court system.) While admitting that "this case is obviously destined to go higher," the district judge confined his consideration to the narrow legal and geographic context of the dispute: "Upon the facts the case really comes down to the provisions of the ordinance, certain physical facts characterizing the situation as it affects plaintiff's land, and the nature and extent of the impairment of its value by the ordinance restrictions."[25] The court found that

> the normal and reasonably-to-be-expected use and development of plaintiff's land along Euclid Avenue is for general trade and commercial purposes, particularly retail stores and like mercantile establishments; . . . the evidence also clearly shows that the restrictive provisions of the ordinance in question impaired the salability of this land and depressed its present market value to the extent of several hundred thousand dollars.[26]

The court then sought to determine whether this economic detriment to the private owner could be justified in terms of appropriate objectives of the police power, namely, to protect the "public health, safety, and welfare." The court found the public objectives of the zoning law, viewed at the municipal scale, to be improper:

> The plain truth is that the true object of the ordinance in question is to place all the property in an undeveloped area of sixteen square miles [in Euclid] in a strait-jacket. The purpose to be accomplished is really to regulate the mode of living of persons who may hereafter inhabit it. In the last analysis, the result to be accomplished is to classify the population and segregate them according to their income or situation in life. [27]

The court also found the ordinance to serve an "esthetic purpose," namely, "to make this village develop into a city along lines now conceived by the Village Council to be attractive and beautiful." [28] It held such a motive to be irrelevant to the claimed benefits of alleviation of congestion. Euclid's zoning law was accordingly declared "wholly null and void."

The village then appealed the case to the U.S. Supreme Court. The implications of this appeal for the hundreds of municipalities that had already adopted zoning were apparent. According to the village attorney, James Metzenbaum: "It was recognized from coast to coast, that a defeat in this case would cause all zoning ordinances in successive order throughout the land to fall, like a row of dominoes stood on end." [29] Euclid thus became the constitutional test case for zoning.

In rehearing the case, the Supreme Court allowed Alfred Bettman to file a brief as "friend of the court" on behalf of the National Conference on City Planning. Bettman's brief has been widely credited with reshaping the Court's perception of zoning and thus gaining its constitutional approval. Bettman sought to shift the Court's attention from the immediate circumstances of *Euclid* and the plaintiff's property to a broader consideration of national trends in urban development and the need to mitigate "the evil effects of unregulated building development in urban communities in America." [30] Citing numerous prior decisions upholding selective application of the police power to regulate individual activities, Bettman instead advocated an approach "based upon a full and comprehensive study of the developments of modern American cities, with full consideration of economic factors of municipal growth, as well as the social factors." [31]

The crux of Bettman's argument was that the physical congestion and deterioration of American cities are a danger to public health, safety, and welfare that can most effectively be addressed through zoning based on city planning:

> Disorderliness in environment has its detrimental effect upon health and character as disorderliness within the house itself. . . . The

essential object of promoting what might be called orderliness in the layout of cities is not the satisfaction of taste or aesthetic desires, but rather the promotion of those beneficial effects upon health and morals which come from living in orderly and decent surroundings.[32]

The Supreme Court agreed with Bettman. After reciting the basic facts of *Euclid,* it ignored them entirely in its decision and adopted the broad national perspective urged by Bettman:

Building zone laws are of modern origin. They began in this country about twenty-five years ago. Until recent years, urban life was comparatively simple; but with the great increase in concentration of population, problems have developed and constantly are developing, which require, and will continue to require, additional restrictions in respect of the use and occupation of private lands in urban communities.[33]

The Court agreed that zoning need not be limited to the literal regulation of nuisance, although "the law of nuisances . . . may be consulted not for the purpose of controlling, but for the helpful aid of its analogies in the process of ascertaining the scope of, the power."[34] In a much-quoted phrase, the Court stated that "a nuisance may be merely a right thing in the wrong place — like a pig in the parlor instead of the barnyard."[35] The Court made no effort to resolve whether Ambler Realty's proposed use of its land would amount to a "pig in the parlor." Instead, it deferred to the opinions of "commissions and experts" that segregation of land uses through zoning based upon comprehensive studies promotes the public health, safety, and welfare and is therefore constitutional in principle.

While thus upholding the validity of zoning as an institution, the Court left open the possibility that the application of zoning may be found to be "arbitrary and unreasonable" in individual cases. Thousands of subsequent lawsuits have in fact challenged the application of zoning laws under particular sets of geographic facts, with diverse results.

Zoning as an institution is entrenched in American land use law. Nevertheless, since the mid-1960s zoning has generated much criticism. The thrust of this concern is that contrary to the theory of zoning as an instrument of comprehensive planning, it has in fact been exercised at a narrow geographic scale to promote the parochial objectives of individual municipalities. Arguably, the Supreme Court in *Euclid* was unduly swayed by a vision of zoning that was functionally unachievable in light of the fragmented political geography of U.S. metropolitan areas. It was to be at least four decades, however, before the issue of exclusionary zoning in the face of regional housing needs would be raised.

Exclusionary Zoning: "Whose General Welfare?"

Probably no land use policy issue has generated more controversy than the use of zoning by local municipalities to exclude unwanted types of development and, by implication, certain socioeconomic groups.[36] The problem arises from the long-standing tradition that zoning is strictly a municipal function, exercised under authority delegated by the state. Zoning enabling acts specify procedural requirements for the adoption and administration of zoning but provide little policy guidance. Furthermore, since the time of *Euclid,* municipal zoning measures have enjoyed the presumption of validity in the absence of proof that they are arbitrary or capricious. Given some semblance of a plan or planning process, zoning provisions are generally upheld upon appeal to the courts.

But the premise that zoning derives its constitutional validity from its basis in planning fails to address the scale at which such planning is conducted. As early as 1927, Bettman recognized a potential danger in the administration of zoning on a purely municipal basis: "Insofar as the fact of the location of a municipality within a metropolitan urban area has a bearing upon . . . development trends, land values, and appropriateness of use, such fact has a relation to the social validity and, consequently, in the last analysis, to the constitutional validity of the zone plan."[37] Nevertheless, local governments have long been notoriously self-centered in the administration of their zoning laws. In 1972 John Reps wrote:

> Zoning regulations are intensely parochial. Standards required in any single metropolitan area vary enormously depending on the whims of local legislatures. We make much of the principle that land similarly located must be similarly zoned within a given municipal body. But this concept is clearly violated when a homogeneous area is zoned for industry on one side of a municipal boundary line and for high-cost, low-density residential uses on the other side. The possibility of achieving coordinated and balanced metropolitan development under such a situation, as far as land-use regulation is effective at all, can be written off as a mere fiction.[38]

Parochiality in zoning has involved several interrelated local objectives, such as (1) reduction of local property tax burdens, (2) preservation of environmental quality and open space, and (3) maintenance of socioeconomic homogeneity. The first two objectives, which are socially and legally justifiable, may be explicit, while the third objective, which is constitutionally suspect, may be implicit. The methods also vary: Large minimum lot sizes and street frontage requirements and limits on multifamily dwellings are the most common forms of exclusionary zoning. The evolution of judicial attitudes toward these restrictive measures further reflects the role of geographic perception of judges in the interpretation of constitutional doctrines.

Euclid did not involve exclusionary zoning per se: Minimum lot sizes were minuscule by modern standards, and two-family dwellings were allowed in the zone classification to which the plaintiff objected. Nevertheless, the Court went out of its way to disparage apartments in single-family residence districts:

> With particular reference to apartment houses . . . the development of detached house sections is greatly retarded by the coming of apartment houses, which has sometimes resulted in destroying the entire section for private house purposes; that in such sections the apartment house is a mere parasite, constructed in order to take advantage of the open spaces in attractive surroundings created by the residential character of the district. . . . Under these circumstances, apartment houses, which in a different environment would be not only entirely unobjectionable but highly desirable, come very near to being nuisances.[39]

The Court thus viewed the issue at the scale of the neighborhood or block, not the municipality or region. The thrust of its dictum is that segregation of housing types, like segregation of residential from nonresidential activities, is constitutionally valid in the interests of preserving safe and healthy single-family neighborhoods. It apparently did not occur to the Court that multifamily dwellings might be totally excluded from countless suburban municipalities under this rationale. Nor did apartments have the association with "affordable housing" that they assumed in the 1960s. However, perhaps with Bettman's guidance, the Court left open the "possibility of cases where the general public interest would so far outweigh the interest of a municipality that the municipality would not be allowed to stand in the way."[40]

Surprisingly few cases addressed the metropolitan or regional context of zoning until the 1960s. In 1949 the New Jersey Supreme Court in *Duffcon Concrete Products, Inc.* v. *Borough of Cresskill* upheld Cresskill's ban on industry, stating:

> What may be the most appropriate use of any particular property depends not only on all the conditions, physical, economic and social, prevailing within the municipality and its needs, present and reasonably prospective, but also in the nature of the entire region in which the municipality is located and the use to which the land in that region has been or may be put most advantageously.[41]

The court noted the availability of industrial land near but outside Cresskill's corporate area of jurisdiction. Haar cited the above as "probably the best judicial statement on regional planning."[42]

The principle was restated in *Borough of Cresskill* v. *Borough of Dumont,* in which three neighboring boroughs challenge Dumont's rezoning for a small shopping center on a single parcel that coincidentally abutted the boundaries of all three plaintiff jurisdictions. In response to Dumont's assertion that "the responsibility of a municipality for zoning halts at the municipal boundary lines," the court stated:

Such a view might prevail where there are large undeveloped areas at the borders of two contiguous towns, but it cannot be tolerated where, as here, the area is built up and one cannot tell when one is passing from one borough to another. Knickerbocker Road and Massachusetts Avenue are not Chinese Walls separating Dumont from the adjoining boroughs. At the very least, Dumont owes a duty to hear any residents and taxpayers of adjoining municipalities who may be adversely affected by proposed zoning changes. . . . To do less would be to make a fetish out of invisible municipal boundary lines and a mockery of the principles of zoning.[43]

Ironically, both of these decisions were exclusionary in their implications. One holds that a municipality *may* and the other that it *must* exclude land uses that conflict with the interests of adjoining areas. The reverse principle, that communities may not exclude land uses to the detriment of the surrounding region, was not raised directly until a series of key decisions emerged from the courts of Pennsylvania and New Jersey beginning in the mid-1960s.

The "large lot" approach to exclusionary zoning was considered in the 1965 Pennsylvania decision of *National Land and Investment Company* v. *Kohn*. This case involved a challenge by a developer against a 4-acre minimum lot size imposed by Easttown Township. In striking down this requirement, the court utilized a two-pronged geographical analysis. On the one hand, it cited and detailed the township's regional setting:

The Township finds itself in the path of a population expansion approaching from two directions. From the east, suburbs closer to the center of Philadelphia are reaching capacity and residential development is extending further west to Easttown. In addition, a market for residential sites is being generated by the fast-growing industrial-commercial complex in the King of Prussia-Valley Forge area to the north of Easttown Township.[44]

In the face of such prospective regional demand for housing, the court noted that 47 percent of the land area of Easttown was zoned for either 2- or 4-acre minimum lots.

On the other hand, the court rejected the town's contention that a 4-acre requirement was necessary to serve "alleged public purposes" concerned with sewage, water supply, roads, and "rural character." The court found inadequate functional connection between the requirement and these objectives. It concluded that the 4-acre requirement was invalid and admonished the township:

Zoning is a tool in the hands of governmental bodies which enables them to more effectively meet the demands of evolving and growing communities. It must not and cannot be used by those officials as an instrument by which they may shirk their responsibilities. Zoning is a

means by which a governmental body can plan for the future — it
may not be used as a means to deny the future.[45]

The same court repeated this statement in 1970 in *Appeal of Girsh,* which
involved prohibition of apartments. The Pennsylvania court thus signaled its
recognition that the nature of suburbanization was changing. No longer simply
bedrooms for central-city executives, suburbs were increasingly attracting jobs,
thereby creating a demand for a wider range of housing opportunities. According to these cases, suburbs that welcome new commercial investment may not
use zoning to avoid the burden of accommodating new residents and building
types: "As long as we allow zoning to be done community by community, it is
intolerable to allow one municipality (or many municipalities) to close its doors
at the expense of surrounding communities and the central city."[46]

The Pennsylvania cases thus chipped away at the underpinnings of exclusionary zoning by attacking two of its basic approaches, apartment bans and over-
sized lots. Although rhetorically recognizing the regional context of zoning,
these cases did not directly address the responsibility of local governments to
contribute to meeting regional housing needs at all income levels. (The units
proposed in *Girsh* were in fact luxury apartments.)

The burden of carrying the rationale of the Pennsylvania cases to its logical
conclusion was assumed by the New Jersey Supreme Court in *Southern Burlington
County NAACP v. Township of Mount Laurel.* The court's opinion, by Justice Frederick Hall, provided an unusually detailed description of the geographical setting
and policy context. According to Hall, Mount Laurel circa 1975 was a flat, sprawl-
ing, 22-square-mile rural township of mixed development and farming located
within commuting distance of Camden, New Jersey, and Philadelphia. Between
1960 and 1970, its population more than doubled to 11,221. Most of the vacant
land remaining at the time of the lawsuit was zoned for industry. Like the U.S.
Supreme Court in *Euclid,* the New Jersey court clearly intended this to be a major
policy declaration, not confined to the narrow circumstances of *Mount Laurel*:

> The implications of the issue presented are indeed broad and far-
> reaching, extending much beyond these particular plaintiffs and the
> boundaries of this particular municipality.
> There is not the slightest doubt that New Jersey has been, and con-
> tinues to be, faced with a desperate need for housing, especially a
> decent living in accommodations suitable for low- and moderate-
> income families.[47]

The court skillfully specified the geographic scope of its decision. It neither
was limited to the defendant township nor encompassed the entire metropolitan
area or state. Instead, the court addressed

> municipalities of sizeable land area outside the central cities and older
> built-up suburbs of our north and south Jersey metropolitan areas . . .
> which, like Mount Laurel, have substantially shed rural characteristics
> and have undergone great population increase since World War II, . . .
> and remain in the path of inevitable future residential, commercial
> and industrial demand and growth. Most such municipalities . . .
> present generally comparable physical situations, courses of municipal
> policies, practices, enactments and results, and human, governmental,
> and legal problems arising therefrom. It is in the context of communi-
> ties now of this type, or which may become so in the future, rather
> than with central cities or older built-up suburbs or areas still rural
> and likely to continue to be for some time yet, that we deal with the
> question raised.[48]

This specification of a particular subclass of municipalities, differentiated in terms
of location, demography, and stage of development, comprised an unusual example of judicial discernment of geographic context. Having set the geographic
stage, the court continued to its legal findings:

> *Mount Laurel* has acted affirmatively to control development and to
> attract a selective type of growth . . . and . . . through its zoning ordi-
> nances has exhibited economic discrimination in that the poor have
> been deprived of adequate housing and the opportunity to secure the
> construction of subsidized housing and has used federal, state, county,
> and local finances and resources solely for the betterment of middle
> and upper income persons.
>
> There cannot be the slightest doubt that the reason for this course
> of conduct has been to keep down local taxes on *property* . . . and that
> the policy was carried out without regard for non-fiscal consider-
> ations with respect to *people,* either with or without its boundaries.[49]

The opinion raised explicitly the constitutional question of whose general
welfare must be served or violated in the field of land use regulation. The court
answered its own question by declaring that the constitutionality of zoning
requires that in the case of "developing municipalities": "Every such municipality must, by its land-use regulations, presumptively make realistically possible an
appropriate variety and choice of housing . . . at least to the extent of the
municipality's *fair share of the present and prospective regional need.*[50]

Mount Laurel precipitated an imbroglio involving the New Jersey courts,
municipalities, legislature, and governor in legal strife that continues to the
present time. The crux of the problem was that the court, having ordered developing municipalities to revise their zoning laws to provide opportunity for low-
and moderate-income housing, lacked the resources and administrative capability
to enforce this mandate. In particular, the concepts of "region," "developing
municipality," and "fair share" lacked specificity. Numerous delaying tactics were
employed by affected communities:

New Jersey municipalities were not ready to give in. They found many excuses for delaying and fudging the court's order. Many of the municipalities against whom suits were brought to challenge their regulations under *Mount Laurel* claimed they were not "developing," and in some cases, they won. Other municipalities, such as Mount Laurel itself, rewrote the ordinances purporting to comply, but in fact only giving the appearance of complying. Still others pleaded that the available land was environmentally sensitive and pointed to Hall's blessing in *Mount Laurel* of efforts to save New Jersey's ecology.[51]

In 1983 the New Jersey court issued a sequel decision in *Southern Burlington County NAACP v. Township of Mount Laurel*. The court declared that it was "more firmly committed to the original *Mount Laurel* doctrine than ever" but recognized a "need to put some steel into that doctrine."[52] In a level of detail more characteristic of a legislature or the federal courts, the New Jersey court articulated a series of policies and standards for the resolution of the myriad *Mount Laurel* cases then clogging the state's lower courts. Amid further lawsuits protesting this action, the New Jersey legislature in 1985 adopted a fair housing act that codified the judicial approach with some modification. This act was upheld in a third major decision in the *Mount Laurel* series: *Hills Development Company v. Somerset County*.[53]

Mount Laurel and its progeny technically apply only to New Jersey. The U.S. Supreme Court declined to review the original decision since it was based on state constitutional grounds. In November 1988, however, the Court in *NAACP v. Huntington, New York*[54] upheld a lower court decision that invalidated the refusal of a municipality to zone land for subsidized housing in an all-white neighborhood. The Court thus came full circle from its *Euclid* position that apartments are a "mere parasite" in single-family neighborhoods. It implicitly recognized that its essentially architectural statement in *Euclid* had long become a pretext for racist and economic exclusion. The path–breaking recognition of the geography of regional housing markets in the Pennsylvania and New Jersey cases was thus ultimately sanctioned by the U.S. Supreme Court.

CONCLUSION

This chapter has briefly examined the geographical context of some key judicial land use decisions. The three pairs of decisions on nuisance, the police power, and zoning, respectively, and the longer series concerned with exclusionary zoning display marked shifts in legal outcome within each set. Where the "facts" of a case remain identical (as in *Euclid*) or very similar (as in *Hulbert* and *Boomer* and *Mahon* and *Keystone*), it is conventional to ascribe differences in judicial result to reinterpretation of common law or constitutional principles. The alternative hypothesis suggested here is that the legal principles remain the same but the facts do "change," at least in the perception of the judges. This formulation is consistent with the Supreme Court's dictum in *Euclid* cited earlier:

> While the meaning of constitutional guarantees never varies, the scope of their application must expand or contract to meet the new and different conditions which are constantly coming within the field of their operation. In a changing world, it is impossible that it should be otherwise. . . . A degree of elasticity is thus imparted, not to the *meaning,* but to the *application* of constitutional principles.[55]

It is not only the world that changes but also the judicial perception of the world as influenced by arguments and briefs of opposing counsel (particularly "friends of the court," as in *Euclid* and *Mount Laurel*) and by the judges' personal knowledge. The change in legal result in each of the sets of cases discussed reflects a refinement of judicial recognition of the geography of the controversies in terms of spatial organization, scale, function, and externalities. In *Boomer, Keystone, Mount Laurel,* and the Supreme Court opinion in *Euclid,* the common denominator is the willingness of the deciding court to consider the broader regional and socioeconomic implications posed by a specific land use case, in contrast with earlier decisions addressing identical or similar issues in a narrow geographic context. Courts certainly differ in their propensity to engage in such "judicial activism," as do legal scholars on the desirability of such a judicial role. Nevertheless, the apparent relationship between geographic perception and legal result underscores the opening assertion of this chapter, that collaboration between the disciplines of law and geography in land use cases is inevitable.

NOTES

1. R. J. Johnston (1984), *Residential Segregation; the State and Constitutional Conflict in American Urban Areas.* London: Academic Press.

2. Brian J.L. Berry (1967), *Geography of Market Centers and Retail Distribution* (Englewood Cliffs, New Jersey: Prentice Hall); Brian J.L. Berry and William L. Garrison (1958), "The Functional Bases of the Central Place Hierarchy," *Economic Geography,* 34, pp. 145-154; Risa Palm (1981), *The Geography of American Cities* (New York: Oxford University Press).

3. J. W. Reps (1972), *Tidewater Towns: City Planning in Colonial Virginia and Maryland.* Charlottesville: University of Virginia Press.

4. J. M. DeGrove and N. E. Stroud (1987), "State Land Planning and Regulation: Innovative Roles in the 1980s and Beyond," *Land Use Law,* 9, pp. 3-8; J. A. Kusler (1985), "Roles Along the Rivers: Regional Problems Meet National Policy," *Environment,* 27, pp. 18-44.

5.   *Village of Euclid* v. *Ambler Realty Co.,* 272 U.S. 386 (1926).

6.   *Hulbert* v. *California Cement Company,* 118 P. 928 (1911).

7.   *Hulbert* v. *California Cement Company,* op. cit. at 930.

8.   *Hulbert* v. *California Cement Company,* op. cit. at 932.

9.   *Hulbert* v. *California Cement Company,* op. cit. at 930.

10. *Boomer* v. *Atlantic Cement Company,* 257 N.E. 2d. 870 (1970).

11. *Boomer* v. *Atlantic Cement Company,* op. cit. at 871.

12. *Pennsylvania Coal Company* v. *Mahon,* 260 U.S. 393 (1922).

13. *Pennsylvania Coal Company* v. *Mahon,* op. cit. at 413.

14. *Pennsylvania Coal Company* v. *Mahon,* op. cit. at 415.

15. *Pennsylvania Coal Company* v. *Mahon,* op. cit. at 413.

16. *Pennsylvania Coal Company* v. *Mahon,* op. cit. at 416.

17. *Pennsylvania Coal Company* v. *Mahon,* op. cit. at 417–418.

18. *Keystone Bituminous Coal Association* v. *DeBenedictus,* 107 S.Ct. 1232 (1987).

19. *Keystone Bituminous Coal Association* v. *DeBenedictus,* op. cit. at 1243.

20. *Keystone Bituminous Coal Association* v. *DeBenedictus,* op. cit. at 1236–1237.

21. *Keystone Bituminous Coal Association* v. *DeBenedictus,* op. cit. at 1243.

22. S. Toll (1969), *Zoned American.* New York: Grossman Publishers.

23. A. Bettman (1946), *City and Regional Planning.* Cambridge: Harvard University Press, p. 159.

24. *Ambler Realty Company* v. *Village of Euclid,* 297 F. 307 (N.D. Ohio, 1924).

25. *Ambler Realty Company* v. *Village of Euclid,* op. cit. at 308.

26. *Ambler Realty Company* v. *Village of Euclid,* op. cit. at 309.

27. *Ambler Realty Company* v. *Village of Euclid,* op. cit. at 316.

28. *Ambler Realty Company* v. *Village of Euclid,* op. cit. at 316.

29. Toll, op. cit., p. 230.

30. Bettman, op. cit., p. 193.

31. Bettman, op. cit., p. 173.

32. Bettman, op. cit., p. 173.

33. *Village of Euclid* v. *Ambler Realty Co.,* op. cit. at 386.

34. *Village of Euclid* v. *Ambler Realty Co.,* op. cit. at 387.

35. *Village of Euclid* v. *Ambler Realty Co.,* op. cit. at 388.

36. C. M. Haar (1955), "In Accordance With a Comprehensive Plan," *Harvard Law Review,* 68, pp. 1154–1175.

37. Bettman, op. cit., p. 55.

38. Reps, op. cit., p. 32.

39. *Village of Euclid* v. *Ambler Realty Co.,* op. cit. at 394.

40. *Village of Euclid* v. *Ambler Realty Co.,* op. cit. at 390.

41. *Duffcon Concrete Pproducts, Inc.* v. *Borough of Cresskill,* 64 A.2d. 347 (1949) at 349–350.

42. C. M. Haar (1963), "The Social Control of Urban Space," in *Cities and Space,* edited by Lowdon Wingo Jr. Baltimore: Johns Hopkins University Press, p. 204.

43. *Borough of Cresskill* v. *Borough of Dumont,* 104 A.2d. 441 (1954) at 445.

44. *National Land and Investment Company* v. *Kohn,* 215 A.2d. 597 (1965) at 605.

45. *National Land and Investment Company* v. *Kohn,* op. cit. at 610.

46. *Appeal of Girsh,* 263 A.2d. (1970) at 399.

47. *Southern Burlington County NAACP* v. *Township of Mount Laurel,* 336 A.2d. 713 (1978) at 716.

48. *Southern Burlington County NAACP* v. *Township of Mount Laurel,* op. cit. at 717.

49. *Southern Burlington County NAACP* v. *Township of Mount Laurel,* op. cit. at 723 (emphasis original).

50. *Southern Burlington County NAACP* v. *Township of Mount Laurel,* op. cit. at 726.

51. *Southern Burlington County NAACP* v. *Township of Mount Laurel,* op. cit. at 724 (emphasis added).

52. *Southern Burlington County NAACP* v. *Township of Mount Laurel,* 456 A.2d. 390 (1983) at 410.

53. *Hills Development Company* v. *Somerset County,* 456 A.2d. 621 (1986).

54. *NAACP* v. *Huntington, New York,* 57 Law Week 1011 (1988).

55. *Village of Euclid* v. *Ambler Realty Co.,* op. cit. at 386 (emphasis original).

6

GEOGRAPHY, LAW, AND MINERAL DEVELOPMENT

OLEN PAUL MATTHEWS

Decisions to develop mineral deposits are based on several factors. Physical variables such as ore grade, ore volume, and depth below the surface can affect these decisions, as can economic variables like market size and transportation costs. Law has increasingly become a variable in the decision process either by raising developmental costs or by restricting development on specific sites. Many in the mineral industry believe that environmental laws make mineral development prohibitively expensive. Thus law is viewed as a geographic variable influencing the location of mineral development. Links between mineral law and geographic as well as economic concepts have become increasingly important.

Many laws impact land use and mineral development. Some, including most environmental laws, are applied uniformly within the United States. Other laws affecting mineral development explicitly incorporate spatial variation. For example, mineral development is prohibited or limited in national parks, wildlife refuges, and wilderness areas.

Mineral development is also linked closely to land status, "the relationship or circumstances one stands in with regard to property."[1] Land status usually refers to ownership or control of both the land surface and the minerals for a particular site. Ownership gives a person rights to use, possess, and dispose of property. This right is not absolute because a property owner cannot commit illegal acts or create a nuisance.

The Mining Law of 1872, which is still valid after more than 120 years, provides the statutory method for establishing this property right on federal land. Not all public land is subject to the 1872 mining law, resulting in restricted "development ability" for this land. Thus "the range of choices available to a property owner depends upon the nature and extent of the ownership interest which he holds, as much as the physical and locational aspects of his land."[2]

Laws governing land status relationships may place the control of the surface and the minerals in the hands of different entities. For example, the federal government may own the surface and an individual may own the minerals.

A state can own the surface, the federal government the coal, and an individual the "other" minerals. With the addition of each type of owner or controller, the law becomes increasingly complex. Even on federal land one agency may control the surface resources while another controls the minerals.

Uniform laws apply to mineral development regardless of location. Typical are those federal laws related to taxation, health and safety, and the environment. Within the United States, these laws are "neutral" with regard to mineral development because they are applied to all people on an equal basis. Acquiring mineral rights on private and state lands usually requires different processes which may include purchase of mineral rights (or the entire surface and mineral estate) or some type of leasing arrangement. Minerals on federal lands may be obtained under a patenting process, through a lease, or by purchase. The exact process used depends on either the status of the land or the type of mineral. Minerals of low value can only be purchased, regardless of the federal land type on which they are found. Fuel and fertilizer minerals can only be leased. On the outer continental shelf and on acquired lands, only leases can be obtained. If land is "open public domain," a patent on valuable mineral deposits may be possible if all the required statutory steps are taken. This last method of obtaining rights is the subject of considerable controversy and one reason for amendments currently being proposed in Congress.

This chapter looks first at the "uniform" laws impacting mineral development and then turns to the complex spatial variations resulting from land status. A case study of the Cabinet Mountains wilderness is presented as an example of the legal restrictions associated with mineral development.

UNIFORM LAWS — LAW AND LANDSCAPE

Uniform laws that have an impact on mineral development include federal tax laws, federal safety and health laws, and federal environmental laws. During the 1970s a deluge of federal environmental legislation resulted in hundreds of pages of regulatory and statutory material. As one source noted in 1984, "Today the Environmental Protection Agency alone has more than 5000 pages of regulations implementing these statutes, and has a backlog of many years' work assigned to it by Congress."[3]

Environmental laws have a direct impact on mineral development through the permitting process. The most important federal environmental laws include the National Environmental Policy Act (NEPA); the Clean Water Act; the Clean Air Act; the Resource Conservation and Recovery Act; the Surface Mining Control and Reclamation Act; the Comprehensive Environmental Response, Compensation, and Liability Act; the Federal Land Policy and Management Act; the Endangered Species Act and other wildlife protection statutes; the Toxic Substances Control Act; the Antiquities Act; the Archaeological

Resources Protection Act and other cultural protection statutes; the Atomic Energy Act; and the Coastal Zone Management Act.[4] Many of these statutes require mineral developers to submit environmental impact statements before mining actually begins.

The process of obtaining environmental permits for a mining project in which an environmental impact statement is required may take between fifteen months and five years. The permitting process usually begins during the exploration phase of development in order to avoid later delays. At this point, although millions of dollars may have been spent, final decisions on such things as mill sites, milling and metallurgical processing, tailings disposal sites, scale of operations, or even whether the mine will be on the surface or underground may not have been made. Each of these decisions will have different impacts on the environment and will involve different environmental laws. The "job of identifying necessary environmental permits is fundamentally a legal one requiring the application of a large and rapidly changing body of law to the facts of the mining activities involved."[5] Agencies have considerable discretion in how laws are applied, complicating the process considerably; "uniform" laws may not be applied equally under all circumstances. Differences between specific projects coupled with different interpretations of appropriate statutes can affect the permitting process dramatically.

The nature of a project will change during this developmental phase depending on the results of exploration, technical studies, the economic picture, and environmental constraints. Even though exact details are not known, the permitting process must begin to avoid delays and the expenses associated with them. Companies generally give a range of production levels and alternative developmental plans in order to get the process started.

Which permits are actually required depends on many site-specific features. For example, a mine close to a wilderness area may require an air-quality permit. Some developments may be exempt from certain air-quality permits if they emit fewer than 250 tons per year of designated pollutants.

MINING LAW AND LAND STATUS

Most mining companies have land departments that make the land status determination for mining projects. Generally, this is done before exploration has progressed very far. Money spent on land not open for acquisition and development is money wasted. In order to understand land status and the problems associated with it, we begin this section by exploring background information on the evolution of mineral ownership in the United States. After discussing the evolution of mineral ownership, we turn to the acquisition of federal minerals.

The Evolution of Mineral Ownership

The transfer of British common law to North America resulted in modification. Modification was especially critical in the case of land and property law, for "land law was the kernel and core of common law. More exactly, real property law was the core."[6] Power, wealth, and status in England had been based on rights in land, which was a relatively scarce commodity. In North America, in contrast, no gentry evolved, and land was abundant and widely held. Thus attitudes toward land were different.

Under English common law, surface ownership included mineral ownership, except for "royal mines," areas where ancient customs controlled, and instances where surface and mineral ownership had been severed by private parties.[7] The "royal mines" included gold and silver, with the Crown owning an interest in all such deposits. Other minerals could be privately owned.

In England local customs were recognized in Cornwall, Devon, Derbyshire, and the Forest of Dean.[8] These local customs often gave a free right of access to mine if certain procedural steps were followed. Also, English common law allowed the land's surface to be sold while part or all of the minerals were withheld, or the minerals themselves could be sold: "Thus one person might be entitled to the iron and another to the limestone. One seam or stratum of coal in the same lands might belong to a third person and another distinct seam to a fourth owner."[9] Problems associated with this type of severed estate are common in the United States.

Most of the colonial charters contained reservations of a percentage of royal metals; 20 percent was common. The states formed after the Revolution did not assert the royal prerogative, and gold and silver reverted to the surface owners. New York is the exception, with the state retaining all gold and silver as well as non-citizen-owned "other" minerals.[10]

After the Revolution, a major change occurred in U.S. land law. The Treaty of Paris had granted the newly independent United States sovereignty over the lands between the Atlantic and the Mississippi River. Although the thirteen colonies claimed sovereignty over much of the sparsely inhabited territory west of the Appalachians, they ceded these territorial claims to the federal government during the 1780s. These federal lands were augmented by other lands acquired by government purchase.

During this early period, Congress attempted to treat mineral lands differently from agricultural lands. The Land Ordinance of 1785 reserved an interest in "one-third part of all gold, silver, lead and copper mines, to be sold, or otherwise disposed of as Congress shall hereafter direct."[11] This reservation was invalid after the Continental Congress ended. No real mineral policy existed in the United States because minerals were not a major issue in the late 1700s. Mineral lands were sold like other federal property.

Following the Louisiana Purchase in 1803, the lead mines in Missouri became part of the United States. Later discoveries of lead in the galena district along the upper Mississippi River and copper on the south side of Lake Superior led to the sale of most of these mineral resources. This occurred even though mineral lands were reserved from the agriculture land disposal laws. Lake Superior copper was sold to the highest bidder.[12] A lease system attempted in Missouri and the galena district between 1807 and 1829 was a failure because of poor administration and pressure on the land by miners and farmers. Even during the period when leases were required, sales of mineral lands took place under agricultural statutes. Sales of mineral lands were eventually authorized in specific areas, including the upper Mississippi lead district and the copper district of upper Michigan and Wisconsin.

These early mining districts were plagued with problems of insecure titles. Lead had been mined in Missouri in the early 1700s, with title to some mines having been granted under Spanish and French law. Prior to the 1807 reservation of mineral lands, the United States sold minerals in the district as well. Thus some mines were private, others were leased, some were simply mined by trespassers, and others were sold as agricultural land. The mines operating on this frontier were not completely without law, and attempts were made to create secure titles for mineral properties. Local mining codes existed in Wisconsin in the 1830s and Iowa in the 1840s. Local codes were needed because "settlement had run past the borders of legitimate government."[13]

In 1830, for example, five miners in the Dubuque, Iowa, area drew up regulations for new mines. The miners themselves lived on the east side of the Mississippi River because land on the west side belonged to the Sac and Fox Indians until the 1833 Blackhawk purchase.[14] The miners were trespassers in 1830, but the rules they established recognized valid titles within the group and group enforcement of rights. This organization, like the agricultural claim clubs,[15] allowed transfers of "property rights" before title was actually granted. The regulations limited each mining claim to 200 square yards and required each to be worked at least one day in six.[16]

When the California gold rush started in 1849, the mining community was familiar with the old English customary law. Meanwhile Spanish mining law had penetrated into California. English and Spanish law thus formed the basis for the laws that evolved during the gold rush. The local mining codes developed along the upper Mississippi River were precedents for the mining codes that evolved in the West. But no federal mining law existed to give miners the right to take minerals from the public lands. In fact, the miners were trespassers like their predecessors in Iowa.[17] The system of property rights that evolved was respected and enforced by the miners in the camps. The miners were not as lawless as sometimes depicted, and a legal system based on customary practice was developed to give secure title to mineral property. These customary practices eventually became federal law.[18]

A federal mining law was passed in 1866 and amended in 1870 and 1872 to become the Mining Law of 1872.[19] At this time the three major land categories — federal, state, and private — had mineral acquisition methods associated with them. Because mineral ownership can be severed from surface ownership, odd combinations of federal, state, and private lands were also in existence.

Private land, both fee simple (one owner) and severed estates, was controlled by the evolving common law of property and contracts.[20] Each state has its own common law and has enacted statutes modifying common law. The result is spatial variation among state laws. States were also granted land at statehood and through other federal programs giving states mineral ownership.[21] Although states have different mineral acquisition systems, leases are the most common. The procedures for obtaining a lease also vary spatially from state to state. About one-third of the United States remains in federal hands. Most of this land is in twelve western states. Because much of it has mineral potential, the federal system is critical in understanding mineral acquisition. The next section discusses acquiring federal minerals and the problems associated with the federal system.

The Acquisition of Federal Minerals

There are several general steps within the federal acquisition process, beginning with determination of land status. If a mineral developer follows the steps necessary to establish a federal right but the land is owned privately or by the state, time and money are wasted because no federal rights can be established.

Federal land status can be determined by examining Bureau of Land Management (BLM) master title plats, graphic records derived from the official survey plats, and surveyor's notes.[22] Using over 150 abbreviations and 20 symbols, these plats show all land transferred from federal ownership as well as any retained federal rights. The plats contain information on the four categories of federal land — open, acquired, withdrawn, and reserved — and the outer continental shelf. If the land has a mineral lease, supplemental plats show the location. Existing mining claims can be found from a geographic index.

The four status categories on federal lands control the acquisition process. Any process may be used on open public domain. Acquired land and the outer continental shelf are not available for patents. If land is classified as reserved or withdrawn, no development may be allowed or the development may be restricted in some way.

On open public domain, three processes can establish mineral rights: patents (location system), lease, and purchase. The process depends on mineral type and value. Any of the three processes may be on reserved or withdrawn land. On acquired land all "valuable" minerals must be leased and "common" varieties purchased. Only leases are possible on the outer continental shelf.

When the 1872 Mining Law was passed, federal land that had not been transferred to states or private individuals was considered public domain, free and open for mineral development. Altogether, 1,838 million acres, or 79.3 percent of the entire United States, became federal.[23] Over 658 million acres of this land remains in the hands of the U.S. government, which has also acquired other land. Acquired land was once in private or state ownership and was subsequently acquired by the government. Many of the eastern national forests are under this category, as are many scattered small tracts surrounded by open public domain. In 1984 the federal government owned over 67 million acres of acquired land which is not subject to the 1872 law.

Since 1872 some public lands have been withdrawn or reserved from mineral entry. Each reservation or withdrawal must be examined individually to determine what prohibitions apply. In 1968 only 17 percent of the federal land had been withdrawn or reserved as national parks, military reservations, wildlife refuges, and other areas. By 1974 over 60 percent was restricted, including withdrawals under the Alaska Native Claims Settlement Act and wilderness study areas under the Wilderness Act.[24] Not all this land is still subject to withdrawals, and more may be released. A little over one-third of federal land is still restricted.[25]

In 1983 President Ronald Reagan signed into law the Outer Continental Shelf Act.[26] This law affected the U.S. exclusive economic zone, the area that international law reserves exclusively for resource exploitation by Americans. The act extended the zone to 200 miles from the coastline, placing almost 2 billion acres under federal control.[27] Regulations are being developed for mining nonenergy minerals on the outer continental shelf.[28]

The open public domain is the most complex category with all three acquisition methods present. "Location" or "locate" refers to the method of patenting mineral rights under the 1872 Mining Law. The law states that "all valuable mineral deposits in lands belonging to the United States both surveyed and unsurveyed, shall be free and open to exploration and purchase."[29] For almost fifty years, the 1872 Mining Law was almost the only law regulating federal mineral acquisition. In 1920 specified fuel and fertilizer minerals were changed to a lease system. The law was changed again in the late 1940s and the mid-1950s. Abuses to the system were recognized because of claims being staked on sand, gravel, and other common mineral materials. Other common varieties were not available because they weren't considered valuable; these materials were converted to a purchase system.

Under the 1872 Mining Law, a citizen can acquire rights to valuable minerals on the public domain by accomplishing certain acts of "location."[30] Federal law supplemented by state law requires the following in most western states:

1. discovery of a valuable mineral deposit
2. posting a location notice on the ground
3. marking the claim on the ground
4. discovery work or its statutory equivalent
5. filing a location notice with the county recorder and state BLM office

The discovery of a valuable mineral deposit is the most difficult requirement. The rule is generally stated as follows: "Where minerals have been found and the evidence is of such a character that a person of ordinary prudence would be justified in the further expenditure of his labor and means with a reasonable prospect of success in developing a mine, the requirements of the statute have been met."[31] The Supreme Court has interpreted this to mean the minerals must be capable of being sold at a profit.[32] The "prudent person" and "marketability" tests are the standards used to determine valid discoveries. Until a discovery is actually made, a mining claimant is protected from all but the federal government by the judge-made concept of *pedis possessio,* or protection of the claimant's rights prior to the actual discovery of valuable minerals.[33]

Today's prospectors generally finish all steps needed for a claim before a discovery is made. Years of exploration may be needed before it is proven a claim can be marketed at a profit. In order to have a valid discovery, minerals must exist on each claim.[34] The mere presence of a mineral is not enough; a mineral deposit must exist — and how much mineralization constitutes a deposit is unclear. If a deposit does exist, however, its size can be estimated by using geologic inference. Geologic inference cannot be used for small amounts of low-grade materials because they are not deposits.[35] There must be a market for the deposit.[36] Costs — including development costs, transportation, environmental protection, easements, water rights, and financing — must be considered.[37] The price the mineral will sell for is also relevant.[38] The market price of a mineral at the time of its withdrawal is the relevant price in the case of withdrawals. In other cases the historic range of a mineral's value is used to determine the price.[39]

Other requirements for marking claims, posting notice, and discovery work vary according to state law. The 1872 Mining Law allows local and state law to control some aspects of claim staking. In general, claim posts must be put at each claim corner, but some states require additional end posts or side posts. Some states require a post at the discovery point. Claim notices are posted at the discovery point or on one of the corner posts. Claim notices usually contain the name of the claim, the name of the claimant, the date the claim was discovered, the type of claim, and a legal description of the claim boundaries. Although discovery work is no longer required on claims in all states, a map of the claim's location may be required as a substitute. Historically, a hole 6 feet by 6 feet by

10 feet deep had to be dug on each claim. Claim notices must be recorded with the county recorder where the claim is located, as with all real property interests. Since 1976, claimants have been required to file a notice and map with the state BLM office.

Four different claim types are possible: lode, placer, tunnel, and mill site. Each of these claims gives slightly different rights. The biggest problem is distinguishing between lode and placer claims. Lode claims are valid only for "veins or lodes of quartz or other rock in place." Placer claims involve anything that is not a lode. In the early part of the twentieth century, petroleum was considered a placer deposit because it was not "rock in place." Lode claims are rectangles with a maximum size of 1,500 feet by 600 feet. Placer claims are 20-acre squares laid off according to the public land survey system. The size and shape of lode and placer claims were historically controlled by local mining districts, resulting in some of the contorted shapes present on maps today. Staking a lode claim gives no rights to placer minerals nor placer claims to lode minerals. Tunnel claims are rarely used but give rights to 1,500 feet along veins found while digging a tunnel. Mill site claims have no mineral rights and convey only a right to use the surface for milling purposes. Lode, placer, and mill site claims can be patented.

Claims can be developed without being patented. To maintain an interest in a claim, however, $200 worth of work must be done on each claim every year. This "assessment work" must be recorded with the state BLM office, or the claim is invalid. The type of work required and where it must be performed is not always clear.

Unpatented mining claims give mining claimants certain rights: They may use the surface of the claim for mining purposes, but they cannot exclude others.[40] Claimants also have extralateral rights, which give claimants a property interest in any vein that surfaces on their claims. They can follow the dip of a vein even when it goes under other property as long as the vein is federal property. These rights are limited to the downward extension of the vein between the claim's projected end lines. Frequent problems occur because end lines are not parallel or because the vein did not dip in the assumed direction.

The Mineral Leasing Act of 1920 is the first modern law controlling leasable minerals on the open public domain. Coal, phosphate, sodium, oil, oil shale, and gas were included in the 1920 act. Sulfur, potassium, additional fuel minerals, and geothermal resources were added later. Today separate regulations exist for oil and gas, geothermal resources, coal, and other solid minerals. The federal government retains a property right in leasable minerals and is paid rentals and royalties. As with locatable minerals, leases will be given only for minerals that exist in "commercial quantities," similar to the test used to determine if locatable minerals are valuable. Competitive and noncompetitive leases can be issued.

For a noncompetitive lease, a developer can obtain a prospecting permit and go exploring. If a valuable mineral is found, the developer can get a lease. Leasing is generally considered discretionary, so developers do not have free access as they do with locatable minerals. Before leases are granted, environmental assessments are made, and leases may be denied for environmental reasons. The lease process has many more procedural steps before a property right is established.

The third method of obtaining mineral rights is by purchase. Sand, gravel, cinders, clay, and other common varieties of mineral materials are usually sold at fair market value. Although these materials are valuable, they are not subject to the location or lease systems unless they are unique in some way. Procedures have been established by the surface management agency for obtaining these materials, including sales to the private sector after competitive bids and free use to nonprofit and government entities.

The discussion above is simplified and brief. To recap: On the open public domain all three acquisition methods are used. Acquired land is not open for mineral location, but the lease and purchase system is the same as on "open" land. On the outer continental shelf, only leasing is allowed, usually by competitive bid. Withdrawn lands may or may not be restricted.

WITHDRAWALS: THE CABINET MOUNTAINS EXAMPLE

Lands classified as wilderness or wilderness study areas provide a good example of the problems associated with withdrawn lands. Within the boundaries of the Cabinet Mountains wilderness area of western Montana, two world-class silver deposits have been discovered. Although many mineral developers quit all exploration in wilderness or wilderness study areas, limited development is possible.

Mining in wilderness areas seems to be a contradictory concept.[41] However, Congress, in a compromise to pass the Wilderness Act, allowed new mining claims to be established in wilderness areas until December 31, 1983. Any claim valid on that date may continue and carries with it development rights. A valid discovery as discussed above must have existed on December 31, 1983. The ability to explore and develop in wilderness areas has limitations, as developers in the Cabinet Mountains discovered.[42]

In 1979 ASARCO began exploration drilling on a block of claims mostly within the boundary of the Cabinet Mountains wilderness area. The initial results were encouraging, and ASARCO filed a plan of operations that would cover the four field seasons prior to the closure of the wilderness on December 31, 1983. After an environmental assessment, the Forest Service approved the company's exploration plan but added stipulations to protect wilderness values and grizzly bear habitat. With a major exploration program approved, ASARCO was set for the next four years.[43]

In January 1981 a small mining company, Eldorado Gold and Silver, staked 176 claims north and east of ASARCO's claim block.[44] Eldorado tried to get ASARCO to buy or lease the claims, but ASARCO was not interested. U.S. Borax — or, rather, their exploration subsidiary, PCMI — leased the claims in 1981 after referring Eldorado to ASARCO. During the 1981 exploration season, PCMI located 99 additional claims partially overlapping the claims they had leased. PCMI also staked 168 claims west and 108 claims south of ASARCO, but most of these were outside the wilderness. By the end of the 1981 exploration season, PCMI had completed all the steps necessary to establish valid claims except discovery of a valuable mineral deposit. A discovery, as discussed above, requires more than the mere presence of mineralization; to be valid, each claim needed a mineral sample as a minimum requirement. Because the deposits in this area are mostly buried, an extensive drilling program was necessary. PCMI's exploration program was hampered by the wilderness classification, the presence of an endangered species, and the existing ASARCO operation. With endangered species the cumulative impact of activities is considered. Anything PCMI proposed had to be considered an addition to ASARCO's approved activity. If a full environmental impact statement had been required, PCMI would probably have terminated the project because the delay would not have given it time to make a discovery before the wilderness was closed.

The plan of operations PCMI submitted requested permission for a maximum of nine drill holes in 1982 and fourteen in 1983. Following an environmental assessment, the Forest Service approved the plan of operations with modifications. A major obstacle was the impact on grizzly bear habitats. After consultation with the U.S. Fish and Wildlife Service, the Forest Service granted approval with stipulations: No camping near drill rigs was allowed, roads were closed, and helicopter corridors and flight times were controlled.

During the 1982 season, U.S. Borax began drilling and staked additional claims in the area as geologic information was available. Two zones of stratified ore were found relatively late in the season. The 1983 plan developed by PCMI would continue exploration on the two zones discovered and on two additional targets, one of which was outside the wilderness. An updated plan of operations was approved for the site outside the wilderness and the ones with mineralization that had been approved in 1982.

PCMI had to get additional approval for its new target within the wilderness. Three sites were to be drilled, and if indications warranted, six drill rigs would be added in order to drill up to twenty-five holes. The company submitted an operating plan on November 29, 1989. Because exploration would occur in a new area, the Forest Service initially reacted negatively. On January 5, 1983, PCMI modified the plan, but it was still unacceptable. After considerable negotiation with the Forest Service and formal consultation with the Fish and Wildlife Service, the company finally developed a plan that allowed one hole to be drilled in the new target area. PCMI began drilling on August 3 but encountered no mineralization.

As part of the process of getting approval to drill the hole, PCMI had to buy out an ongoing logging operation and the Heidelberg Mining Company's exploration operations: Reducing the impact of these two operations would lessen the total cumulative impact on the grizzly bear enough to allow PCMI to proceed. In order to get Heidelberg to stop operating, PCMI agreed to do some work on its claims. In early August, while geologists were inspecting the Heidelberg claims, they scanned some rock bluffs with their field glasses and found a copper-stained outcrop 2,500 feet away, near Rock Lake. Prospectors filed sixty claims on this discovery during August and September.

On August 25 PCMI applied for permission to drill up to four holes behind the outcrop. Equipment and supplies were to be carried by hand around Rock Lake. Drilling was approved for November 11 through November 15. Two holes were drilled, confirming the mineralization. The Forest Service approved a third hole on December 1.

After receiving the assay reports from these holes, PCMI requested permission for exploration in December. PCMI was under a deadline. On December 31, 1983, wilderness areas would close and only valid claims could continue. The Forest Service rejected the proposed drilling because of potential harm to grizzly bears. Although mineral discoveries had been made in several areas, PCMI was not certain the claims would be considered valid.

While the Forest Service was making its validity determination, it defined the exact wilderness boundary around Rock Lake. The outcrop and the two holes drilled in November 1983 were outside the wilderness. The Forest Service approved twenty days of drilling in late August 1984 on the claims outside the wilderness, and the resulting work confirmed a north-dipping stratiform silver and copper deposit. In February 1985 the Forest Service determined that 4 of the 202 Rock Lake claims straddling the wilderness boundary were valid. Using the doctrine of extralateral rights, the agency included the vein's extension under the wilderness to the north. The Forest Service allowed later development drilling in the wilderness in areas above the vein and off valid claims and approved three drill sites that were to be supported from a camp within the wilderness. The camp, including walkways, was built on wooden platforms to reduce impacts on vegetation. In 1986 a similar program of development drilling went forward, with four sites being drilled. The drilling showed a continuous vein extending at least 8,400 feet from the discovery outcrop. The U.S. Borax deposit within the wilderness area consists of 250 million tons of ore worth several billion dollars in place.

In 1988 U.S. Borax and its partners sold their interest to Noranda and a consortium of others for a total of $93 million. Noranda is in the process of driving a tunnel from a patented claim 18,000 feet east of Rock Lake outside the wilderness. ASARCO is also attempting to get approval for its holdings. If U.S. Borax had discovered the Rock Lake deposit later, it is doubtful the company would have been able to drill its exploration holes prior to December 31, 1983. Without the holes a valuable mineral deposit could not have been proven, and Borax would not have been able to sell the deposit for the considerable sum it received. Changing land status would have stopped future exploration.

CONCLUSION

The law controlling the development of mineral deposits is a complex mix of federal and state law. The process of acquiring mineral rights begins with land status because status determines the legal process to be followed. U.S. Borax had many more complications in the Cabinet Mountains wilderness than it would have had if its discovery of a mineral deposit had been completely outside the wilderness area. But it also had an advantage: Because part of the discovery was outside the wilderness, additional drilling was allowed in 1984 that would not have been permitted otherwise. By good fortune the company was able to find sufficient mineralization so a mineral deposit could be said to exist. Once the existence of a deposit was established, geologic inference could be used to determine the extent and value of the deposit. The doctrine of extralateral rights allows the vein to be followed under a wilderness area where no valid claims exist. If the mineral discovered had been leasable, it would have been valueless because leases were not being issued in wilderness areas during this time.

"Uniform" laws also had an impact. Many of the problems U.S. Borax encountered can be attributed to the Endangered Species Act rather than wilderness classification. Because the cumulative impact of all activities had to be considered in approving any activity, U.S. Borax had to pay others to reduce activity in order to complete its own exploration drilling. Even then, the way the drilling was conducted, the drilling season, and other aspects of the exploration were strictly controlled by law.

Reforms to the Mining Law of 1872 have frequently been proposed. In the summer of 1994, two competing provisions were put before Congress. The Senate version, sponsored by Senator Larry Craig (R.-Idaho), is the industry-supported reform. Under this proposal the patent process will continue, but those obtaining a patent will have to pay fair market value for the surface rights. This is designed to prevent a claim from being patented and then turned into some other use, such as a ski resort. In addition, a 2 percent royalty, determined after deducting costs, would be required on those claims staked after the law is passed.

The House version, sponsored by Representative Nick Rahall (D.-W.Va.), is supported by the environmental community. This bill eliminates patents completely, imposes an 8 percent royalty on the gross value produced on existing and future claims, requires that areas be restored to a condition capable of supporting the same activities as before mining, and allows the surface management agencies to withdraw areas that they determine to be unsuitable for mining. Compromise has yet to occur, with several major issues still unresolved and the political muscle to make significant change missing. Even if reform is enacted, however, the legacy of the Mining Law of 1872 will continue, and existing valid mining claims will be constitutionally protected property rights.

NOTES

1.   *Black's Law Dictionary* (4th edition) (1968). St. Paul: West Publishing Company, p. 1580.

2.   Rutherford H. Platt (1976), *Land Use Control: Interface of Law and Geography.* Washington, D.C.: Association of American Geographers.

3.   Chery Outerbridge (1984), *American Law of Mining.* New York: M. Bender.

4.   National Environmental Policy Act, 42 United States Code, §§4321–4327 (1988); Clean Water Act, 33 United States Code, §§1251–1376 (1988); Clean Air Act, 42 United States Code, §§7401–7642 (1988); Resource Conservation and Recovery Act, 42 United States Code, §§6901–6987 (1988); Surface Mining and Reclamation Act, 30 United States Code, §§1201–1328 (1988); Comprehensive Environmental Response, Compensation and Liability Act, 42 United States Code, §§9601–9657 (1988); Federal Land Policy and Management Act, 43 United States Code, §§1701–1784 (1988); Endangered Species Act, 16 United States Code, §§1531–1543 (1988); Toxic Substances Control Act, 15 United States Code, §§2601–2629 (1988); Antiquities Act, 16 United States Code, §§431–438 (1988); Archaeological Resources Protection Act, 16 United States Code, §§470 (1988); Atomic Energy Act, 42 United States Code, §§2011–2246 (1988); Coastal Zone Management Act, 16 United States Code, §§1451–1465 (1988).

5.   Outerbridge (1984), op. cit.

6.   Lawrence M. Friedman (1985), *A History of American Law* (2nd edition). New York: Simon and Schuster.

7.   Curtis H. Lindley (1897), *Lindley on Mines.* San Francisco: Bancroft Whitney.

8.   Nicholas J. Campbell Jr. (1957), "Principles of Mineral Ownership in the Civil and Common Law Systems," *Tulane Law Review,* 31, pp. 303–312.

9.   Lindley (1897), op. cit.

10.   Lindley (1897), op. cit.

11.   Paul W. Gates, ed. (1968), *History of Public Land Law Development,* written for the Public Land Law Review Commission. Washington, D.C.: U.S. Government Printing Office, p. 65.

12.   Swenson (1968), op. cit.

13.   Friedman (1985), op. cit.

14.   Jesse Macy (1884), *Institutional Beginnings in a Western State.* Baltimore: Johns Hopkins University Press.

15.   Allen G. Bogue (1958), "The Iowa Claim Clubs: Symbol and Substance," *Mississippi Valley Historical Review,* 45, pp. 231–253.

16.   Macy (1884), op. cit.

17.   Joseph Ellison (1963), "The Mineral Question in California," in *The Public Lands,* edited by Vernon Carstensen. Madison: University of Wisconsin Press, pp. 71–92.

18.   John P. Reid (1980), *The Law for the Elephant: Property and Social Behavior on the Overland Trail.* San Marino, California: Huntington Library.

19.   Mining Law of 1872, 30 United States Code, §§22–51 (1982).

20.   Outerbridge (1984), op. cit.

21.   Olen P. Matthews (1985), *Legal Pitfalls, Land Status and the Acquisition of Mineral Rights* (2nd edition). Moscow: Idaho Mining and Mineral Resources Research Institute.

22.   Howard L. Edwards (1967), "The Silk Purse and the Sow's Ear: Benefits and Limitations of the Project to Improve the Federal Land Records," *Rocky Mountain Mining Law Institute Proceedings,* 12, pp. 243–267; W. Frank Meek (1971), "Federal Land Office Records," *University of Colorado Law Review,* 43, pp. 177–197; Verl C. Ritchie (1973), "Title Aspects of Mineral Development on Public Lands," *Rocky Mountain Mining Law Institute Proceedings,* 18, pp. 471–492.

23.   Marion Clawson (1971), *The Bureau of Land Management.* New York: Praeger, p. 7.

24.   Alaska Native Claims Settlement Act, 43 United States Code, §§1601–1628 (1988); Wilderness Act, 16 United States Code, §§1131–1136 (1988).

25.   Outerbridge (1984), op. cit.

26.   Outer Continental Shelf Act, 43 United States Code, §§1331–1343 (1988).

27.   Robert W. Smith (1981), "Maritime Boundaries of the United States," *Geographical Review,* 71, pp. 395–410. The figure used by Smith is 2,222,000 square nautical miles for the area adjacent to the fifty states.

28.   Outerbridge (1984), op. cit.

29.   Mining Law of 1872, 30 United States Code, §22 (1988).

30.   Outerbridge (1984), op. cit.

31.   *Castle v. Womble,* 19 I.D. 455 (1894) at 457.

32.   *United States v. Coleman,* 390 U.S. 599 (1968).

33.   Terry N. Fiske (1969), "Pedis Possessio — Modern Use of an Old Concept," *Rocky Mountain Mining Law Institute Proceedings,* 15, pp. 181–216.

34.   Kathryn Toffenetti (1985), "Valid Claims in Wilderness Areas," *Land and Water Law Review,* 20, pp. 31–66.

35.   *United States* v. *Feezor,* 74 IBLA 56 (1983); *United States* v. *Hooker,* 48 IBLA 22 (1980).

36.   *Melluzo* v. *Morton,* 534 F.2d 860 (9th circuit, 1981).

37.   *United States* v. *Pittsburgh Pacific Corp.,* 30 IBLA 388 (1977); *United States* v. *McKenzie,* 4 IBLA 99 (1971).

38.   *United States* v. *Hooker,* 48 IBLA 22 (1980).

39.   *In re Pacific Coast Molybdenum Co.,* 75 IBLA 16 (1982).

40.   *United States* v. *Curtis Nev. Mines,* 415 F.Supp. 1373 (E.D. Cal., 1976).

41.   Olen P. Matthews, Amy Haak, and Kathryn Toffenetti (1985), "Mining and Wilderness: Incompatible Uses or Justifiable Compromise?" *Environment,* 27, pp. 12–21.

42.   Donna J. Loop (1986), "Claiming the Cabinets: The Right to Mine in Wilderness Areas," *Public Land Law Review,* 7, pp. 44–69.

43.   The approval process was not completely smooth. The Forest Service went to court for failure to comply with NEPA and the Endangered Species Act; see *Cabinet Mountains Wilderness/Scotchman's Peak Grizzly Bears* v. *Max Peterson,* 510 F.Supp. 1190 (1981); affirmed, 685 F.2d 678 (1982). The case was eventually settled out of court.

44.   Stephen Goss (1987), "Land Status and Other Geographic Factors Affecting a Mineral Exploration Project," M.A. thesis, Department of Geography, University of Idaho.

7

FORENSIC GEOGRAPHY, LEGAL GEOMORPHOLOGY, AND PRACTICAL GEOJURISPRUDENCE[1]

ERNEST S. EASTERLY III

Geographers are playing increasingly important roles in the legal process as expert witnesses and scientific consultants. Yet the published literature on the subject of forensic geography, or the direct application of geographical information and expertise to legal proceedings, remains regrettably sparse.[2] Moreover, the potential contribution of geographers to legal proceedings has often been overlooked in favor of representatives of less-qualified disciplines. Civil engineers and land surveyors have frequently been appointed as expert witnesses in legal proceedings, though they often lack the training in political geography, historical geography, cartography, and geomorphology necessary to provide adequate levels of information to the judicial system.

Accordingly, geographers must define the nature and scope of forensic geography, articulate its essential paradigms and principles, outline the basic practices of the field, and encourage the use of professional standards in the application of geographical knowledge to the resolution of legal questions. The purpose of this chapter is to illustrate the value of geography as a discipline in the legal process. Hypothetical and actual case studies illuminate the role of a geographical perspective in legal proceedings.

Geographers who venture into forensic geography must avoid the temptation of entering the realm of lawyers as advocates and rhetoricians. The nature of the adversarial process of our legal system, together with the court's need for technical input, characterizes the forensic geographer's role as largely educational in style and content. Geographers induced to apply their expertise in legal negotiations and litigation, therefore, should remember that the only legal reason for serving as an expert witness is to help adjudicatory bodies find the truth in a given case by the orderly presentation of facts and methods.

THE MARINE BOUNDARY NEGOTIATION SEQUENCE

The process of determining marine boundaries provides an excellent illustration of the forensic role of geography. Boundaries between states, counties, and other jurisdictions have long been subject to dispute in the United States. Parties to a boundary dispute often attempt to reach agreement out of court. In the absence of such agreement, legal proceedings may be initiated to settle the dispute. In either case determining the boundary requires evidence and expertise provided by geographers and geomorphologists. A review of a suggested boundary negotiation sequence, therefore, provides a valuable example of forensic geography.

Many boundaries pass through lakes, bays, sounds, or other bodies of water. Water boundaries are generally described less carefully and thoroughly than boundaries on land. For purposes of this discussion, we assume that the land boundary between two jurisdictions is undisputed and accurately delineated. Resolution of a dispute involving a boundary extending into a body of water begins by tracing the known land boundary to the edge of the lake, bay, or sound. An example might be the extension of the known land boundary between Illinois and Wisconsin into Lake Michigan.

In other cases the boundary approaches the lake, bay, or sound by way of a stream. For example, the boundary between Texas and Louisiana enters the Gulf of Mexico by way of the Sabine River. Under these circumstances the boundary extends to the stream-closing line, or the line that continues the general curvature of the shores across the mouth of the stream, unless the thalweg, or main navigable channel of the stream, extends into the larger body of water. In that case the boundary will generally follow the thalweg.[3]

In the absence of a well-defined channel of deep water, the larger body should be closed by a line across the stream mouth. That line should be drawn from the two points where the riverbank turns to become the shoreline of the larger body.[4] If the boundary approaches the lake, bay, or sound along one bank of the stream, the boundary should be extended to the closing line, following the trend that it had where it met the shoreline of the larger body. In any event the advice of geographers and geomorphologists should be solicited to determine the exact location of the boundary.

Once the place where the boundary reaches the inland margin of the larger water body has been determined, reference must be made to the document that allocates territory between the jurisdictions. If that document prescribes a boundary that follows some arbitrary (usually straight) line, then the boundary must be drawn as such an arbitrary line through the lake, bay, or sound to the outer terminus, or outermost ending point. If that outer terminus falls on an opposite shore, then the procedure followed in determining the inner beginning point must again be followed in finding the outer ending point. If the document specifies some other stream or pass as the location of the existing boundary, then the thalweg of that stream is determined and used as the point to which the straight or direct line is drawn.

Some allocation documents specify that the thalweg must be followed in determining the water boundary. But if the document uses such language as "through the bay," "with the middle of the lake," or "with the trend of the bay," then three possibilities appear. First, the parties may agree to the use of an arbitrary line. In that case the negotiators should consider carefully and fully the possible difficulties of demarcating that line. These difficulties increase as the number of bends or curves in the boundary increases. Thus arbitrary lines should ordinarily be considered to be a last resort.

Second, negotiators may choose to specify the thalweg, if such a single channel exists, as fulfilling the allocation "through the bay" or any conceptual equivalent. If a single, unambiguous channel crosses the larger water body in the direction indicated in the allocation document, this thalweg is normally selected. If following that thalweg will work a severe hardship upon either those who use the water body or the parties responsible for administering justice upon it, however, a deviation from the thalweg should be devised such as to minimize those hardships.

For example, the natural thalweg may lie very close to one shore, while an artificial navigation channel provides direct access between the main stream and the larger water body. Under such circumstances, a navigator would seem to pass capriciously in and out of the two jurisdictions, while the party that has the boundary near its shore would lack sufficient jurisdiction over the water facing its shore. In such a case, the thalweg should be simplified by placing the boundary in the middle of the artificial channel.

On the one hand, adjustments of this kind are not possible where the allocation document specifies the natural channel. On the other hand, they seem to be mandatory where the boundary has never been delimited and officials of both jurisdictions have for many years treated the artificial channel as though it were the boundary. Careful study of the relevant law, close examination of the facts of nature and of human activities by forensic geographers, common sense, and goodwill should lead the negotiators to reasonable consideration of the special problems of navigation and administration. Geographers can be of considerable assistance in these deliberations.

The remaining possibility available to the negotiators is the Boggs median line, every point of which is equidistant from the nearest point(s) on opposite or adjacent shores. The Boggs median line should be used in any water body having a distinct long dimension, lacking a thalweg, and not allocated according to legislation by some other method. Before the Boggs line is applied, all islands that have some special, historic status must accordingly be assigned to the proper jurisdiction. An example of such a special status is the documented, more or less continuous, unchallenged exercise of jurisdiction over the island by one of the parties.

Consideration should also be given to long-established practices of the people inhabiting the island — as when, for example, they have generally and for long maintained various relations with one jurisdiction but only very little with the other.[5] The boundary should not disrupt the natural community of people in the region of the boundary. Careful research should be carried out to find any relevant information about the motivation for the boundary and any citizens' memorials or petitions concerning the boundary.[6] Newspapers and other records (including those of the courts) should be examined for similar information. Even the opinions of present-day residents may be sought.[7] (It is advisable to retain experts experienced in investigations of customs and the terrestrial localization of laws — hence, practical geojurisprudence proves significant.) But to have a persuasive special status, the island ought to have fairly continuously held its special relation for at least one generation, preferably since the date of the document of allocation.

Having thus agreed upon any island's having special, historic status, the negotiators can ask an engineer or cartographer to prepare a trial map of the boundary by using Boggs's technique and ignoring all islands except the special-status islands. The remaining islands can then be allotted to the parties according to the side they mainly fall within. Then the Boggs line should be drawn again, this time taking account of the newly allotted islands.

Once the Boggs median line has been drawn throughout the water body, the terms of the allocating document have been fulfilled. But if the thalweg line is used for the inner or outer termini of the water body boundary, it will usually be necessary to connect the Boggs line to the thalweg line by a short, arbitrary line, especially where they fail to meet or where they meet in a manner troublesome to the users or the parties involved with the water body.

The boundary having been drawn on the base map (following either the thalweg line, the Boggs line, an arbitrary line, or a combination of these), it should now be described fully in writing. Reference should be given throughout to the laws, principles, evidence, and reasoning for every segment of the boundary. The negotiators should have the cartographer or engineer calculate and provide appropriate geographic description for every point where the boundary crosses a shoreline or changes direction. The engineer should also recommend at this time the kinds and locations of monuments to be used in the demarcation.

PARALLEL HISTORICAL AND
GEOGRAPHICAL CONSIDERATIONS

Throughout this discussion of final negotiations, we have ignored the possibility of historical disputes involving boundaries. Yet there may be disagreement over the historic meanings of place-names and disputes over the locations of features named in the document of allocation. Historical research is often needed to shed light on such disputes. Maps, legal documents, and other sources must be consulted in an effort to identify precisely the intent of those charged with determining the original boundary.

In many cases the conclusion of historical research must be merely the most probable or least unreasonable one, and we greatly increase the chance for honest disagreement — not to mention objections that might arise from ill will or bad faith. How, for example, are we to know what legislators believed or discussed unless we find records of their deliberations? If we know that there were, say, twenty commonly available maps at the date of the act of allocation, how do we determine which map, if any, was used by the legislators? Would the testimony of the majority of the cartographers carry greater weight than the notations of the best of the twenty mapmakers? Can a manuscript map be claimed to have been used by the allocators? What did the legislators believe to be the shape of a certain lake or bay or the name of a particular bayou?

These and similar questions could, if discussed academically, exhaust the patience of the most saintly negotiator. Fortunately, however, most practical historical questions concerning boundaries can be resolved handily if long academic debate is avoided. Most of the abstract problems vanish in the practical instance. To reach practical decisions amicably, the negotiators will have to shift repeatedly between determining the form of the land and water bodies and interpreting the language of the allocation document.

In some cases dispute resolution requires knowledge concerning the shape of the land and water bodies at the date of allocation. These cases can be divided into two groups — cases where factual determination is possible and obtainable at a cost commensurate with the worth at stake; and cases where a factual determination is either impossible or excessively expensive. In either of these cases, the present or some recent map of the features in question may be used as the basis for amicable negotiation. In the second case, such an expedient must be used. Thus if the factual determination is too costly or impossible or if the parties choose simply to accept it, a recent, accurate representation of the shapes — for example, a map prepared by the U.S. Coast and Geodetic Survey — can serve the negotiations well enough to fulfill the law. This practical expedient has the great advantage of saving time and money.

In some cases the body of water will have remained stable in shape, size, and location. Unless great resources are at stake, negotiators should then consider again the possibility of using a recent delineation of the boundary region. If they cannot do so, they should agree to abide by the finding of a competent geomorphologist. The commission to the geomorphologist should contain merely a request for an accurate determination of the shores, banks, and other planimetric outlines of the boundary region; a request for full documentation of the bases for the judgment; and the precise use of place-names from the list of synonyms.

The geomorphologist should not submit opinions as to the location of the boundaries under negotiation. The planimetric outlines prepared by the geomorphologist should appear on the base map in use by the negotiators or upon a present-day map of the boundary region. On account of the great cost of such a determination of the historic shape, size, and location of the features near the boundary, the negotiators should bind themselves to accept the outcome.

While work goes on toward an agreeable map of the shapes, sizes, and locations of the land and water bodies in the boundary region, the negotiators should also face the problem of determining the meanings of the terms, or "calls," in the allocation document. As a first step, the negotiators should prepare a complete list of all calls as they appear and in order. They should also provide copies of the relevant parts of all maps presumed to have been accessible to the legislators (or other allocators), that is, no maps published after the act and probably no general atlas maps. (Most if not all of these maps should already be included in any comprehensive preliminary agreement.)

With very good luck, one and only one of the maps assembled will have all the calls used in the allocation. It is clearly reasonable to presume that the legislators used that map in writing the allocation if every place-name mentioned in the allocation document is matched by the same name for the same feature on that historic map only. If the testimony of historic maps is notably ambiguous, however, the negotiators will have to determine the cartographer most likely to have been followed.

In settling upon the historic map, negotiators will want to keep several principles and facts in mind.[8] Maps based upon direct observation are preferred. The map should have been published (but certainly at least drawn) before the allocation. The part of the map dealing with the boundary region is the main concern (the accuracy of a single map varies from part to part), and the entire region (rather than the water body only) traversed by the allocation must be considered. In general, any map mentioned without prejudice in the document of allocation or in legislation has superior standing.[9]

In evaluating the maps under consideration, negotiators should bear in mind that the original allocation may have been based on more than one map, as well as local knowledge. Place-names may change. Cartographers may make errors, and because most maps are based on other maps, errors may be copied from one map to another. It is also presumed that cartographers living at the time of the original allocation are more knowledegable than their successors.[10] When several allocation documents of different dates pertain, the maps available at each of those dates must be consulted.

If dealing with the question of the most appropriate historic map proves too exasperating or time-consuming for the negotiators (as well it should!), they should retain a historical geographer or historical cartographer to carry out the analysis. Such an arbiter should be familiar with the land and maps of the boundary area so that his or her determination of the boundary can be arrived at accurately, quickly, and inexpensively. The negotiators should instruct the historical geographer to determine the sources of factual information used by the allocators, to state the bases of his or her judgment, and to provide a map showing the most probable intention of the allocators and using their calls.[11]

Having settled upon a historical interpretation of the allocators' intentions, the negotiators should make any indicated adjustments in the list of synonyms, calls, and placements — both actual and generic. All these historical agreements and conclusions should next be integrated into the concurrent efforts to determine the agreeable planimetric outline of the boundary region. Again, unless interests require reconstruction of the historic shoreline, a recent map should be used. In any case the historical geographer's recommendations, together with any geomorphologist's report, must be combined with the agreements of the negotiators into a composite historical recommendation and inserted into the legal negotiation sequence.

Negotiators, however, should keep in mind that they will have to shift repeatedly between legal and historical aspects of the negotiation. Some facts from one topic will influence agreements concerning the other. Some concessions of a point in one area can be matched by concessions in the other. Even so, at all times the active presence of the appropriate geoforensic experts and the geographical evidence they provide should prove virtually indispensable.

A CASE HISTORY

Controversy over the delineation of boundaries in the Lake Pontchartrain basin of Louisiana illustrates the role of the geographer in legal proceedings involving marine boundaries.

These delimitations mark the most complex and comprehensive application of the Boggs median line principle. The simultaneous extension of several boundaries in Lake Pontchartrain, for example, exceeded in both principle and technical application the highly celebrated allocation schemes by the International Court of Justice resulting from the North Sea continental shelf cases, which purport to define national boundaries using the median line, or equidistance, approach. The Lake Pontchartrain delimitations, moreover, take on further relevance for geography in two respects, both reflecting the indelible imprint of geoforensic experts: (1) The delimitation procedure employs the principle developed by the geographer S. W. Boggs as described above, and (2) the articulation of the Boggs median line principle in the Lake Pontchartrain basin reflects the activity of geographers participating in the legal process.

The Lake Pontchartrain basin includes three major bodies of water — Lake Maurepas, Lake Pontchartrain, and Lake Borgne. Although these lakes were once international waters, they are now wholly within the internal waters of the state of Louisiana. The allocation of the basin among the parishes (which in Louisiana are the equivalent of counties) began in 1763, and the subsequent boundary developments begin from that date. The lake boundaries of all parishes that share the basin emerge through a series of territorial additions and subtractions indexed to that first determination of 1763.

Out of a background of vague and conflicting claims among the governments of Spain, France, and Great Britain, the first allocation of the Pontchartrain basin emerged. On February 10, 1763, at the end of the French and Indian War, the British government exacted the Treaty of Paris, which allocated all of North America east of the Mississippi and the land south of the basin (the "Isle of Orleans"). Article 7 of the treaty determined that the boundary between British "West Florida" and the Spanish Isle of Orleans would run through the middle "of the Lakes Maurepas and Pontchartrain, to the sea."

Although this boundary was never surveyed and monumented in a mutually agreeable fashion, the governments accepted and enforced the allocation. This boundary was preserved in subsequent cessions and annexations of territories north and south of the lakes, including the several acts and resolutions admitting Louisiana as a state in the Union. In that way the boundary of 1763 became the boundary of the parishes initially created from the territory of the former British West Florida. This interpretation of the continuing force and validity of the formerly international boundary has been upheld by the courts of Louisiana.

Having noted the necessary historical basis for the determination of the several parish boundaries in the basin, we now turn to a presentation of two resolutions of the delimitation question. The first includes an "academic" solution developed by geographers participating in the legal process (which contrasts remarkably with an unacceptable and wisely rejected proposal presented by land surveyors!). The second reflects the "legislative" solution, which expresses only slight variation from that proposed by the geoforensic experts.

During the time that the academic solution was developed, several parishes sharing jurisdiction over Lakes Pontchartrain and Maurepas met to decide on a resolution of their boundaries. At meetings held from October 1976 to March 1977, geographers were invited to present the historical and theoretical aspects of the boundaries through the lakes. On these occasions, after reviewing the requisite historical analysis, the academic solution based upon the Boggs median line principle was proposed and favorably received. This act proved a significant step in the direction of resolving the correct location of parish boundaries in the lakes, the delimitation of which was the source of much previous confusion.[12]

The earlier confusion was apparently easy to come by. On a map to accompany an unsuccessful attempt in 1943 to set the boundary between Jefferson and St. Charles Parishes, engineers extended the boundaries of St. Charles Parish into the lake to their intersection. To that point, they drew a line from the mouth of Pass Manchac and from the intersection then extended an "axis line" east-southeast well past an extension of the Jefferson Parish boundary with Orleans Parish. They also extended Tangipahoa Parish jurisdiction into the lake, to this "axis line."

The complexity was increased by a 1952 Louisiana Supreme Court decision that allocated revenues from a pipeline extending across the lake and across the awkward tract between the shores of St. Tammany and St. Charles Parishes.[13] The suit and judgment excluded consideration of other parishes that seem to have had claims to the area but were apparently ignorant of their interests in the litigation. But this pipeline, belonging to United Gas Pipe Line Company, provides an excellent test of the consequences of dividing Lake Pontchartrain in one way, the typical engineer–land surveyor approach as opposed to other means of dividing it, such as the academic solution developed by geographers.

Justice Joe B. Hamiter, writing for the court, held "that the boundaries of the parishes of St. Tammany and St. Charles extend to the middle of Lake Pontchartrain."[14] Such a holding is inescapable in the light of either the excellent review written by Justice Hamiter or the historical considerations previously indicated. Yet by the time Justice Hamiter wrote in 1952, Boggs had long since shown that one cannot determine the "middle" of a lake by beginning from the shore.

It seems reasonable enough that if both St. Tammany and St. Charles Parishes extend to the middle of the lake, we could measure the pipeline and divide it in two, leaving one-half in the jurisdiction of St. Charles Parish and one-half in that of St. Tammany Parish. But suppose that another pipeline ran from the northwest shore to New Orleans, and suppose that it were divided at the half-way mark, following the same practice. In this hypothetical case, St. John the Baptist Parish would have taxing authority falling east of part of the United Gas pipeline previously allotted by the court to St. Charles Parish, an awkward situation indeed. Quite obviously, the jurisdictions of two equivalent political units cannot interpenetrate on the whimsical basis that they have half of the jurisdiction over any man-made features originating on their shores. As Boggs pointed out, that is a "landsman's" point of view, and under it no unambiguous solution can be reached.

Instead, Boggs consistently and rather successfully urged the "waterman's" point of view. To determine the jurisdiction over any point in the waters, simply determine which is the nearest land jurisdiction.[15] Thus, for example, from the middle of the United Gas pipeline in Lake Pontchartrain, the nearest land is St. John the Baptist Parish. Even if there had been only two jurisdictions, as was the situation before statehood, the "middle" of the pipeline would have fallen a little northeast of the halfway mark. This would have been, and in fact seems still to be, exactly where the pipeline crosses the boundary of 1763. Thus if we take the waterman's point of view and measure to the nearest land jurisdiction as we progress from point to point along the pipeline, we find a point where the pipeline is equally close to two parishes; that point is the boundary between St. Charles and Jefferson Parishes. This boundary shortens from one-half to less than one-fifth the total lake route of the pipeline lying within the jurisdiction of St. Charles Parish.

The reduction of the share allotted to St. Charles Parish came about, perhaps unexpectedly, because the claims of all adjacent shoreline parishes were exerted simultaneously. Such was made clear by the hypothetical pipeline; the halfway mark would fall well within what is clearly the jurisdiction of Jefferson Parish and east of what, under the decision of the 1952 court, was supposed to be the jurisdiction of St. Charles Parish. In other words, the "middle" seen from the shoreline of St. John the Baptist Parish conflicts with the "middle" as seen from both St. Charles and Jefferson Parishes. As Boggs showed conclusively, the only way to remove the ambiguity of such phrases as "to the middle" is by use of the median line. The median line of 1763, the only line that is equidistant at every point from both the north and south shores, is thus the "middle" or "center" of the lakes.

After nearly two years of deliberations by representatives of the lake parishes, the parishes accepted among themselves the Boggs median line solution presented by the geoforensic experts. The stage was thereby set for legislative intervention in 1978. A bill was introduced portending to establish the parish boundaries on an arbitrary basis, without regard to the Boggs method. Facing adamant opposition from the several parishes of the Lake Pontchartrain Boundary Committee, the legislature determined to defer the proposed boundary act until the next year's session. During the interval, a special Joint Legislative Committee on Parish Boundaries in Lake Maurepas and Lake Pontchartrain conducted hearings and received testimony by representatives of the parishes, legal experts, and expert geographers. As a consequence of these hearings, the previous year's legislative proposals for boundary delimitations were rejected in favor of the Boggs median line proposals by the geographers, which were advocated by the affected parishes. The legislative committee proposed and the legislature passed Act No. 740 of 1979 delimiting the parish boundaries.

Although alike in principle, a brief comparison of the respective maps shows differences in certain minor details between the proposed academic and legislative solutions. Both approaches embrace the Boggs median line principle in the delimitation of parish boundaries through the lakes. The legislative solution, however, presumes to resolve the awkward tract in Lake Pontchartrain claimed by both Livingston and Tangipahoa Parishes in favor of the latter. The matter remains open to potential litigation between the parishes.

Another difference resides in that the legislative solution ignores the thalweg in the eastern end of Lake Pontchartrain. This has the effect of placing the lacustrine thalweg almost entirely within the jurisdiction of one parish, St. Tammany, a result that runs counter to the very essence of the long-standing thalweg doctrine. Beyond these principal differences, minor modifications exist. Yet these modifications reflect technical adjustments rather than substantive alterations. The legislative solution, therefore, reflects to a considerable degree the academic solution developed by geoforensic experts.

The direct participation of geographers as key experts throughout the Lake Pontchartrain boundary delimitation process underscores their worth in boundary determinations. The practical application by professional geographers of such geographical knowledge and expertise serves as the core and basis of the subdiscipline sometimes known as forensic geography. As actors in the drama of delimitation, forensic geographers are able to employ the established means of analyzing prospective boundary problems and subsequently presenting reasonable recommendations to the persons concerned with such boundaries. Such practical guidance provides an exemplary basis for forensic geography.

EXPERTS AND EVIDENCE: GEOGRAPHY ON TRIAL

From the foregoing case studies involving water boundary determinations, the inherent and often indispensable value of forensic geography should be apparent. The same situation prevails in areas other than boundary delimitations, including historic navigability cases, environmental litigation, and land title controversies. Furthermore, although our case studies focused on legal negotiations, the impact of forensic geography is all the more pronounced in the context of actual courtroom proceedings. Many other academic principles may under local circumstances enter into consideration. These include the principles of geography, cartography, geomorphology, ecology, and climatology. Practitioners of these subdisciplines can help determine matters of fact as an aid to the legal process.

The problems surrounding use of these academics and professionals as expert witnesses are vast. There is little doubt that numerous abuses of professional standards have occurred. The current practices concerning the certification of expert witnesses by courts sometimes do not really encourage critical use of the full capabilities of the disciplines commonly used. Hence it is important to consider various warnings and suggestions to the certification and use of expert witnesses.

That some members of a discipline know how to make the determination needed does not mean that they all do. Some geographers have made careful studies of boundaries and boundary drawing, but most have not. It follows that while an expert may claim a unique ability for his or her discipline, no claim to expertise should be accepted without critical examination of actual abilities in each case. Credentials such as doctoral degrees or licenses cannot actually serve to accredit the expert beyond the most minimal levels of competence and credibility. An English-speaking historian may well know more than a French speaker or professor of French about the meaning of French words on an old map, but so may a historical geographer or even an illiterate settler. Although the expert's testimony may be essential to the court where the subject of inquiry relates to some science or art in which persons by study or experience may be supposed to have more skill and knowledge than the trier of fact (judge or adjudicatory hearing officer) may be presumed to have, it should be remembered that even a layperson can testify as to facts within the realm of his or her personal, experiential knowledge.

Likewise, that a discipline commonly deals with one or more aspects of a boundary problem does not mean that followers of that discipline know all other aspects of that problem. Engineers, on the one hand, commonly carry out precise measurements and surveys, but they may lack knowledge to determine what should be measured or surveyed. Geographers, on the other hand, are more likely qualified to evaluate what should be measured or surveyed.

Experts should be required to state the bases of their opinions. Such statements should be expressed in plain language and rendered in step-by-step fashion so that all concerned can follow each element in the reasoning. The court should take the initiative in questioning whenever the attorneys fail to do so.

When an expert's testimony is slanted to such an extent as to preclude any reasonable basis for such opinion, the court should exercise its prerogative of designating an impartial expert in order to create an effective force against the obviously misleading testimony.[16]

Clear and flagrant instances of special pleading by expert witnesses should be punished by the court to the limit of its legal powers. Indeed, the courts should recognize as perjury an expert's stated testimony under oath of a particular opinion or belief that he or she does not really maintain. Such perjury may be evidenced when the expert gives conflicting testimony concerning his or her findings and opinions with no justifiable basis for a change. While the expert may change his or her professional views and opinions, unless there is valid ground for such change, its motivation may be considered corrupt. Any expert advocating one manner of interpretation should be required by the court to give a competent performance of alternate interpretations. A professional should be able to explain clearly and honestly theories and methods that he or she has rejected.

Some questions of fact simply cannot be definitively evidenced by expert testimony. For example, the shape of Grand Lake in south Louisiana has changed greatly over the years. Thus it is unlikely that there can be a conclusively authoritative statement concerning its shape at any point in the distant past. In contrast, we can expect a much more nearly definitive statement on such lakes as Salvador or Catahoula, because their shapes have changed little.

A FINAL RUMINATION

As indicated by the foregoing discussion and case studies on forensic geography, the expert forensic geographer — through careful research and accurate techniques — can be of inestimable value in assisting the court or negotiators in making proper determinations. As James Mitchell has observed, geographers' "ability to interrelate information drawn from varying areal scales and their broad concern for long-term landscape evolution, for the role of unexpected events, and for planned change confer a suite of related perspectives that is usually missing from other analyses of contemporary environmental changes."[17] Even so, a certain amount of professional humility remains in order.

This is well illustrated in the case of *Transcontinental Petroleum Corporation* v. *Texas Company*. In that case, a question of mineral rights and riparian boundaries hinged on whether a stream had been navigable at some time in the past. Both parties retained distinguished geographers of national reputation, who amassed an abundance of facts upon which they articulated well-reasoned theories. The principal legal issue — whether the watercourse had been historically navigable — was approached by the geoforensic experts through recorded evidence, deduction, and analogies. The latter two methods were necessarily highly scientific and specialized yet somewhat inaccurate and therefore incapable of giving a conclusively authoritative determination.

Naturally, there was marked disagreement between the geographers engaged in the dispute. As the court noted in *Transcontinental Petroleum,* both expert geographers successfully advanced theories that developed highly scientific and technical subjects so simply as to be within the grasp of the layperson. Even so, the court rejected the conclusions of both geographical experts. In the fitting words of Justice Amos Lee Ponder, "Whenever it is at all possible . . . courts should refrain from giving to any state of facts the sanctity of judicial decree unless such facts are so strong, positive and convincing as to preponderantly establish the contention as a fact."[18]

Interestingly, the court then decided the case not on the theories of the prominent forensic geographers in the practice of their learned arts but on the testimony of local inhabitants! The moral is simple. The court functions as the sole arbiter of facts. The forensic geographer or expert witness serves as an educator and interpreter of facts. While geographers may be expected to assist the court in discerning truth in the complex intertwining of law and geographical realities, that role remains necessarily limited by both function and facts.

NOTES

1. This chapter is respectfully dedicated to the late Milton B. Newton Jr. (1936–1988), whose contributions to forensic geography merit a separate essay. Parts of this chapter are adapted from two earlier works of mine, Ernest S. Easterly III (1988), "The Role of Geoforensic Experts in Marine Boundary Delimitation: The Case of the Lake Ponchartrain Basin," *Papers and Proceedings,* Applied Geography Conference, 11, pp. 118–124; and Ernest S. Easterly III (1977), *Louisiana Parish Boundaries Through Lakes, Bays and Sounds* (Baton Rouge: Louisiana State University). The balance of the chapter draws heavily from my experiences as special assistant attorney general, administrative law judge, practicing lawyer, qualified expert witness in geography and geomorphology (including before the U.S. Supreme Court), and consultant in more than ninety cases and controversies involving questions of forensic geography, legal geomorphology, and practical geojurisprudence.

2. Examples of recent writings on forensic geography include Louis DeVorsey (1973), "Florida's Seaward Boundary: A Problem in Applied Geography, *Professional Geographer,* 25, pp. 214–220; Louis DeVorsey (1982), *The Georgia–South Carolina Boundary: A Problem in Historical Geography* (Athens: University of Georgia Press); James K. Mitchell (1978), "The Expert Witness: A Geographer's Perspective on Environmental Litigation," *Geographical Review,* 68, pp. 209–214.

3. See *State of Louisiana v. State of Mississippi,* 202 U.S. 1 (1906); *State of Louisiana v. State of Mississippi,* 466 U.S. 96 (1984).

4. Of course this line "closing" the mouth of a river should, like all other determinations based upon a shoreline, be reckoned at mean low water. The reasons for using the low-water mark are discussed by G. Etzel Pearcy (1959), "Geographical Aspects of the Law of the Sea," *Annals,* Association of American Geographers, 49, p. 206. As to how the mouth of a river is to be closed, see G. Etzel Pearcy (1959), "Measurement of the U.S. Territorial Sea," *Department of State Bulletin,* 60 (1044), p. 966.

5. See, for example, *State of Arkansas v. State of Tennessee,* 310 U.S. 563 (1940) at 571.

6. See, for example, *St. Martin Parish* v. *Iberville Parish,* 33 So.2d 671 (1947).

7. See, for example, *State* v. *Texas Company,* 211 La. 326; 30 So.2d 107 (1947); and *Comegys* v. *Stanolind Oil and Gas Co.,* 227 La. 657, 80 So.2d 110 (1955).

8. J.R.V. Prescott (1987), *Political Frontiers and Boundaries* (London: Allen and Unwin).

9. For example, La Tourrette's map (presumably the edition of 1848) was mentioned in Louisiana act 97 of 1850 thus: "The whole of said above line being in conformity to the boundaries of the parish of Terrebonne as laid down by LaTourrette's map of the State of Louisiana."

10. *St. Martin Parish* v. *Iberville Parish,* op. cit.

11. For a very fine example of using a historic map in discovering the legislature's will, see J. P. Morgan (1955), *A Geographical and Geological Study of the Louisiana Coast, With Emphasis on the Establishment of the Historic Shoreline.* Baton Rouge: Louisiana State University Coastal Studies Institute.

12. Ernest S. Easterly and Milton B. Newton Jr. (1976), "Several Parishes Seeking Lake Boundary Agreement," *Louisiana Parish Government,* 12, pp. 22–23.

13. *United Gas Pipe Line Company* v. *Moise,* 220 La. 969, 58 So.2d 197 (1952).

14. *United Gas Pipe Line Company* v. *Moise,* op. cit. at 204.

15. S. W. Boggs (1937), "Problems of Water Boundary Definition: Median Lines and International Boundaries Through Territorial Waters," *Geographical Review,* 27, pp. 445–456.

16. Constance Holden (1989), "Science in Court," *Science,* 243, pp. 1658–1659.

17. Mitchell, op. cit., p. 214.

18. *Transcontinental Petroleum Corporation* v. *Texas Company,* 24 So.2d 248 (1945) at 253.

8

THE REGIONAL EFFICACY OF ENVIRONMENTAL LAW IN MICHIGAN

JEROEN WAGENDORP

In recent years geographers have come to recognize the mutual interests of geography and law.[1] Blacksell has identified the need for increased research in geography and law, arguing that "law as a system of norms cannot be readily understood in language other than that of absolute space, for it possesses a metaphysical quality which simultaneously controls and transcends physical objects."[2]

The emergence of interest in geography and law since the 1970s has been an outgrowth of work by political geographers.[3] A better understanding of the relationship between law and political systems led political geographers to attempt to address the problem of spatial justice. Pirie promoted the notion that "conceptualizing space as a social product rather than as a context for society may yield a substantive concept of spatial justice," while Reynolds and Shelley suggested that local democratic institutions should function in concordance with social justice as derived from societal knowledge, yet be immune from influence by state institutions.[4]

American states, like other political communities, are often characterized by considerable variability in physical environments, economies, and cultures. In the American legal system, however, everybody within a state is subject to the same laws. Few laws take spatial variation in environmental conditions within states into account. Thus laws that may be appropriate for some areas may be completely inappropriate elsewhere. As a result, geographical variation within a state can create substantial regional variation in legal culture or in local attitudes toward the nature and functioning of the legal and judicial systems within that state.

As early as 1939, Whittlesey wrote:

> At the same time they [different legal forms] may produce contrasts on man's use of identical environments. Variations in culture patterns in uniform environments on opposite sides of a political boundary are common, and prove the possibility of modifying the landscape by

political means. The operation of law can be traced only through patient study of incidence of individual laws.[5]

Whittlesey pointed out that relationships among culture, political process, law, and its interpretation are very complex. Addressing these relationships, this chapter investigates the regional differences in the administrative aspects of resource law.

My purpose here is to establish the presence and extent of spatial variation of legal culture in Michigan as reflected by the variations in the enforcement of selected regulatory and statutory environmental laws administered by the Land and Water Management Division of the Michigan Department of Natural Resources. Michigan's attitude toward environmental management has been rather strict and in some cases unique when compared to other states. In 1970 the Michigan legislature passed the Michigan Environmental Protection Act.[6] This law was the first state statute in the United States that explicitly authorized citizen-initiated environmental lawsuits. Similar laws have since been enacted in Connecticut, Florida, Indiana, Minnesota, New Jersey, and South Dakota.[7]

The state of Michigan can be divided into three distinct demographic and socioeconomic regions: the southern Lower Peninsula, the northern Lower Peninsula, and the Upper Peninsula. The southern half of the Lower Peninsula contains the majority of urban areas, economic activity, and as a result the most intensive social and physical infrastructure. The northern half of the Lower Peninsula contains about a dozen cities with a population up to 20,000. The main economic activities include agriculture and tourism located along the coastal regions of Lake Michigan and Lake Huron. The characteristics of the Upper Peninsula, are similar to those of the northern half of the Lower Peninsula but are intensified by geographic isolation from the Lower Peninsula. The social and physical infrastructure is poorly developed. Logging, deer hunting, and tourism are the economic mainstays of this area.

These demographic and socioeconomic regions provide a distinct geographic point of departure from which to begin the analysis. The central research question is whether differences in the efficacy of environmental law can be identified in these distinct regions of the state. "Efficacy" in this context is defined as that which produces the desired effect.

GEOJURISPRUDENCE

Examination of spatial variation in the effects of the law is an aspect of geojurisprudence, or geographic investigation of the study of the law. In this chapter, we define "geojurisprudence" as a geographical extension of the concept of jurisprudence, which for our purposes we may take to be "the name given to a certain type of investigation into law, an investigation of an abstract, general and theoretical nature, which seeks to lay bare the essential principles of law and legal system."[8] Thus it is considered "as a reflection of society's development; as a reflection of developments in legal philosophy; as a reflection of the law's general development; as a social science; and as an exact [but not natural] science."[9]

In addition to these definitions of "jurisprudence," I propose an additional meaning: jurisprudence as a reflection of spatial variation of law, or "geojurisprudence." Wigmore first defined the concept of geojurisprudence and used it to compare the legal systems of the world.[10] This chapter fits within Wigmore's tradition of geojurisprudence, although at a much smaller geographical scale and in a contemporary setting.

The concept of law and culture has traditionally received more attention from anthropologists than from geographers; however, most anthropological studies on culture and law have focused on primitive rural societies.[11] While these studies have advanced a basic understanding of the relationships between law and culture, attempts to apply this perspective in contemporary Western societies have been very few in number. Van Velsen argues that "most writers on African law, with or without legal training have an imperfect understanding of their own legal system with which, explicitly or implicitly, they tend to compare African legal systems."[12]

In the past geographers have dealt with the subject matter of culture and law, but their approaches were often topical in nature, and they provided little information about the regional variation of legal cultures. For example, Pattison investigated the legal background and subsequent development of the U.S. public land survey system (township-and-range system) as a legal survey method responsible for organizing the cultural landscape of the United States.[13] This study was extended by Thrower, who compared the physical development of the cultural landscape under the European metes-and-bounds survey method and the township-and-range system.[14] Others have dealt with the concept of legal culture indirectly and very generally at the global scale, but these studies contribute little to the understanding of regional differences at the national or subnational level.[15]

Three important conceptions underlie Anglo-American law — authority/validity, reasonableness, and historical appropriateness. These conceptions

> rest on a particular, though incompletely articulated, conception of community. It is a *Gemeinschaftlich,* traditionary conception of society, in which the law is regarded as the repository of tradition and a (if not the) primary bond of the community. It is regarded not so much as the sole device for keeping the community from flying apart (as Hobbes regarded it), but as that through which members participate in, and in virtue of which they feel part of, the community.[16]

The concept of reasonableness allows for substantial local or regional variation, for what is reasonable and acceptable in one region might not be reasonable and acceptable in another.

The concept of reasonableness in common law helps to accommodate the spatial variation and uniqueness of law and legal systems. Therefore geography can appropriately play an important role through study of legal culture, since this extralegal material "by law" may have spatial dimensions and since geography has an established and well-endowed spatial-cultural tradition. Additional information on how environmental law interacts within a regional cultural and environmental context will shed new light on other important issues, such as recognizing potential spatial injustices or inequities regarding environmental quality; the distribution of public funds for the administration, compliance, and enforcement of environmental law; and the anticipated outcomes of new environmental regulations and policies.

METHODS

The intent of this chapter is to examine the distribution of legal culture in the state of Michigan and to link this distribution to the distribution of cultural and economic activities in the state. This allowed me to address the following questions: First, if the complexity of the cultural geography in Michigan varies on a regional basis, does the legal culture geographically reflect the complexity of these cultural regions? Or is the legal culture independent of Michigan's cultural geography? Second, because the southern half of Michigan's Lower Peninsula contains a large majority of the state's population and economic development, the physical environment of this region is subject to the most intense stress. Is this region also the target and recipient of the majority of environmental regulation? If so, is this purely the result of population distribution, or are there alternative explanations? Finally, is it possible that the distribution of physical environmental resources, rather than merely the distribution of population, is linked with the pattern and quantity of environmental regulatory activity?

In order to facilitate regional comparison between culture and legal activity, I identified a set of variables representative of cultural activity. These variables included population; real property assessments based on agricultural, commercial, industrial, residential, and timber cutover values; education; per capita income; urbanization; and primary, secondary, and tertiary economic activities. The five different real property tax assessments are representative of cultural activities in different areas. National, state, and local governments recognize these differences, and taxes vary according to the "culturally" perceived or assessed value. For example, real property in a central business district has a higher assessment than a rural cluster of a gasoline station, a grocery store, and a tavern because of its greater rent-generating potential and hence its value.

Within the state of Michigan, agricultural, commercial industrial, residential, and timber cutover land are taxed in accordance with the General Property Tax Act of 1893 as subsequently amended. Assessments are made at the city and township level, equalized at the county level, and approved at the state level by the boards of review. Levels of education, per capita income, and urbanization are also presumed to reflect cultural complexity.

The percentage of the county's labor force employed in the tertiary sector provides additional information about a region's cultural complexity. It measures the intensity of the socioeconomic and political infrastructure, marking the organizational complexity within a given county. The volume of activity in the tertiary sector may also directly relate to the volume and intensity of activity in the primary and secondary sectors.

Each of the variables was measured and mapped across the eighty-three counties of Michigan. A cultural complexity index was then calculated using the formula

$$C = (R^1 + R^2 + R^3 + R^4 + R^5)/P + E/P + I/P + U/P + (Pr/P) \times .04 + (Sec/P) \times .303 + (Tert/P) \times .574,$$

where P is the percentage of the state's population at the county level; $R1$-$R5$ are the percentages of the state's agricultural, commercial, industrial, residential, and timber cutover real property assessments at the county level; E is the percentage of the state's population with sixteen years of education at the county level; I is the percentage of the state's total personal income at the county level; U is the percentage of the state's population living in urban environments at the county level; Pr is the percentage of the state's primary activities at the county level; Sec is the percentage of the state's secondary activities at the county level; and $Tert$ is the percentage of the state's tertiary activities at the county level. The percentages of .04, .303, and .574 reflect the overall percentage of Michigan's employment in the primary, secondary, and tertiary sectors, respectively. Using this index, I calculated a quantitative index of cultural complexity for each of Michigan's eighty-three counties.

I then compared the distribution of cultural complexity as defined above to the distribution of 6,515 permits issued by the Land and Water Management Division of the Michigan Department of Natural Resources. I chose this division for several reasons. First, it forms a daily link between the people of Michigan and the state's environmental management objectives as set forth in the statutes. Second, it is organized geographically within the state in a manner that facilitated regional comparison to other variables. Third, data relevant to daily operations and workload of this division were accessible and inexpensive. Last, my personal experience in previous research made me aware of how important, how imperfect, and how vulnerable a link these administrators can be in the execution of environmental law.[17]

In Michigan public, commercial, recreational, and industrial activities regulated by environmental statutes are administered by the regulatory divisions of the Michigan Department of Natural Resources. This process is facilitated through permits, which are granted or denied on the basis of compliance with environmental regulations. The permitting process originates at the district level. In addition any prepermitting or postpermitting inspections are coordinated and performed by field personnel at the district level. Hence enforcement (volume of permits and inspections) is related to available personnel. For permitting purposes, the state of Michigan is divided into three regions and thirteen divisions.

The volume of permit "traffic" is related to a number of variables not immediately apparent to the outsider, and these vary among the regulatory divisions. For example, involvement with the public at large varies with the nature of the regulations administered. Air pollution, waste management, and surface water quality regulation are largely related to a variety of secondary activities, whereas floodplain, wetland, inland lakes, and erosion control regulations, as administered by the Land and Water Management Division, apply to all human activities alike. Furthermore, public awareness of these regulations has an impact on the permitting volume. Many citizens do not know that a permit is needed for the construction of a seawall or retaining wall in an inland lake or that such a structure might increase or decrease the tax assessment of a given property. A person's awareness of these regulations (or a neighbor who will report new projects) does influence the permitting process, as do attitudes of field personnel and conservation officers of the department.

Environmental violations are observed by field personnel while en route to and from site inspections or work and by conservation officers on patrol. Their action varies: Some will stop and take the appropriate action regardless of time constraints and workload, while others may prefer to ignore new problems. Violators who bypass the permitting process and are reported to the district offices may or may not receive official attention, depending on workload, availability of personnel, and personnel attitudes.

Michigan's Land and Water Management Division administers thirty-one state acts, two executive orders, and nine federal acts. The Land and Water Management Division is fundamentally different from other regulatory divisions of the department in that it is neither resource-specific nor pollution-oriented. Rather than enforcing statutes related to a specific resource (e.g., air or surface water), it enforces a group of statutes that regulate ecological and technical/engineering aspects of land and water use. For example, when a utility company crosses a stream or river with underground utility lines, it must obtain a permit from the Land and Water Management Division. The company has to submit engineering drawings of the site impacted and has to prove that it is in compliance with the applicable statutes. Depending on the site and situation, a typical crossing could involve the Inland Lakes and Streams Act; the Flood, Drainage, and Beach Erosion Act; the Soil Erosion and Sedimentation Control Act; and the Goemaere-Anderson Wetlands Protection Act.[18] When the submitted plan for the crossing complies with the stipulations set forth by these acts and Land and Water Management field personnel have made an on-site inspection, the division issues a permit for the project.

In 1987 the Land and Water Management Division maintained forty persons in the field. They processed 6,515 applications for environment modification in a wide variety of physical settings. The majority (69.4 percent) of these permit applications centered on the Great Lakes Submerged Lands Act[19] and the Inland Lakes and Streams Act.

An analysis of permit applications of previous years shows that the volume statewide more than doubled from 1982 to 1987. The rise in permitting activity during this five-year period can be attributed to an expansion in field personnel staffing; the drastic increase in the levels of the Great Lakes between 1982 and 1987, which required more shoreline erosion protection devices; and the economic recovery of the entire state from the recession of the late 1970s, with a corresponding jump in the number of land development projects. Although the number of permits increased considerably during the 1980s, their distribution across the state has remained fairly constant.

By far the highest permit-to-population ratio was found in the Upper Peninsula. This high ratio is consistent with the high ratio of personnel to population in the region. Among counties in the Upper Peninsula, the permit ratio was highly correlated with the property assessment ratio ($r = +.78$), the commercial real assessment ratio ($r = +.88$), and the residential real assessment ratio ($r = +.86$). However, the correlations between the permit ratio and urbanization and manufacturing were negative. It appears, therefore, that activities outside city limits are regulated by the state. Although abundant in this part of the state, the per capita availability of both rivers and lakes does not show a significant degree of correlation with the number of permits issued.

Region 2, which consists of the northern half of the Lower Peninsula, carried over 25 percent of the total number of permit applications within the state and had 36 percent of the total field personnel allocation. None of the variables investigated for Region 2 showed a significant correlation with this permit ratio. The property assessment ratio and the lake ratio showed a small correlation, a low $r = +.40$. Hence no specific physical environment or human activity draws in these types of state regulations. The regional concentrations of social and economic variables ratios showed negative correlations with the Land and Water Management permit ratio, indicative of cultural complexity in the northern Lower Peninsula.

The southern Lower Peninsula carried 61 percent of the permit applications. The largest ratio was in St. Clair County, the site of the largest, inland freshwater delta in the world. In the southern Lower Peninsula, none of the available variables explains more than 5 percent of the variation of the permit ratios. Only the arrest ratio of the Department of Natural Resources Law Enforcement Division showed a fairly strong correlation, $r = +.53$. This correlation is not apparent for any obvious reason other than that both divisions are active in nonurban areas.

Statewide, the Land and Water Management Division permits were most frequently generated in those counties where the population pressure on lake and forest ratios were rather low. Here the correlation coefficients gained in strength, with $r = +.66$ and $+.43$ respectively. The correlation between the permit ratio and regional concentration of social and economic variables remained negative $r = -.36$.

ENVIRONMENTAL ENFORCEMENT AND LEGAL CULTURE IN MICHIGAN

The analysis described above provided a basis for answering the three questions posed at the outset of the research. The first question asked if the legal culture would geographically reflect the general cultural regions in Michigan. The answer is that it clearly does not. Rather, an inverse relationship appears to exist, with the legal culture very different from the distribution of other cultural activities.

The second question postulated the existence of a positive relationship between the quantity of cultural activity — which resulted in stress on the physical environment — and the quantity of environmental regulation. This relationship is negative. Those areas with the heaviest population pressure on the natural physical environment received the least amount of regulation, while more pristine environments such as those found in the northern Lower Peninsula and the Upper Peninsula were far more heavily regulated.

The last question raised the possibility of a relationship between the unequal regional distribution of regulatory activity and the unequal distribution of the physical resources. These were related positively. The analysis that led to the answer of this question introduces several other unanticipated but crucial findings. Population pressure on the rivers of Michigan is virtually identical with the population pressure on lakes and forests. Where these pressures are highest, the variables representing cultural complexity are also highest. Yet regulation as represented by permit ratios and personnel allocation is lowest in the southern half of the Lower Peninsula.

As a result of poor glacial drainage, Michigan has over 1 million acres of inland lakes (2.76 percent of the state's territory) and over 36,000 miles of rivers and streams. This constitutes an important resource for the state. However, the protection of this resource is concentrated in the northern half of the Lower Peninsula. This is surprising if one considers the lower population pressure on this resource. The southern part of the Lower Peninsula has 652 persons per mile of river, whereas the northern part of the Lower Peninsula has only 91 persons per mile of river and the Upper Peninsula 31 persons per mile of river. But the recreation pressures on the water resources of the northern half of the Lower Peninsula are high. The northern half of the Lower Peninsula has almost 36 percent of the state's lakes — the main attraction for tourists, many of whom reside in the population centers of southern Michigan. In comparison, the southern half has 22 percent of the state's lakes and nearly 90 percent of the state's population.

The distribution of water resources versus people clearly suggests that water-quality law, as reflected by the distribution of permits and personnel, is either severely underenforced in the southern half of the Lower Peninsula or severely overenforced in the northern half. In either case the southern half is the recipient of the least amount of regulation. The heavier-than-anticipated regulation of water resources in the northern Lower Peninsula coincides with substantial recreation pressure from the southern part of the state. In other words, the overall environmental quality in the northern Lower Peninsula is of crucial importance for the maintenance of recreational functions of this area.

This introduces an important conclusion. The legal culture of the northern Lower Peninsula (as far as environmental laws and regulations are concerned) appears not to grow out of local cultural patterns but to have been superimposed by the southern part of the state. Legally and politically, the Upper Peninsula and northern lower Michigan are subject to the objectives generated within more populated and developed southern lower Michigan. Neither the Upper Peninsula nor the northern Lower Peninsula of Michigan possesses sufficient political clout to apply these standardized state environmental statutes according to domestic regional interpretations.

Certain environmental statutes have been written that exemplify this dichotomous situation in Michigan. For example, wetland resources in Michigan are impacted by different environmental regulations in different areas. The Goemaere-Anderson Wetlands Protection Act allows for development of wetlands of less than 5 acres that are not contiguous to inland lakes, streams, or ponds or to the Great Lakes and their connecting waterways in counties with populations of fewer than 100,000 people. The act also contains exemptions for agriculture and lumbering.

The eighteen counties of Michigan that have populations greater than 100,000 are all located in the southern part of the Lower Peninsula. The Goemaere-Anderson Act provides for the protection of all wetlands in these counties, while isolated tracts up to 5 acres in size in rural counties remained open to development. Yet this development is often initiated by pressures from the more urbanized southern part of the state. Population pressure from southern Michigan has rendered wetlands in the northern part of the state less vital for environmental protection. In addition, the state of Michigan controls over 4 million acres of state forestlands in the Upper Peninsula and the northern Lower Peninsula, with the U.S. Forest Service responsible for an additional 2.7 million acres. Logging activities, which can destroy wetlands, are mostly exempted from environmental protection by the Goemaere-Anderson Act.

This dominance of the environmental legal culture superimposed from the south is further sustained by personnel transfers within the Department of Natural Resources. Many employees have transferred from southern lower Michigan to the Upper Peninsula and the northern Lower Peninsula. Not only did these employees leave behind the populated southern part of the state, but they also brought with them certain preconceptions about the environmental destiny of their new place of residence.

This attitude by the south toward the northern parts of Michigan is further illustrated by Sheppard, who described a plan Governor William Milliken proposed in 1971 to zone the northern half of lower Michigan and the Upper Peninsula for preservation and conservation of the physical environment.[20] Although environmentalists hailed it as a way to preserve the undeveloped nature of these regions, Milliken's plan failed because the zoning of an entire state was too controversial in political terms. Ironically, the effects of administration of existing laws wound up closely approaching Milliken's proposal, although in a surreptitious manner. The regional efficacy of environmental law in Michigan is produced by a geographically small portion of the state that contains the majority of the state's population.

This introduces an interesting spatial dichotomy. Is it possible to hold the southern part of the state responsible for environmental imperialism — ensuring access to recreation, resort functions, and tourism as a commodity for the south to enjoy on weekends and during vacations? If this analogy is correct, the regional efficacy of environmental law is in part a vehicle to maintain the environmental status quo in the undeveloped parts of the state.

A similar dichotomy centers on urban versus rural areas. Almost all settlements, especially the larger urban centers of Michigan today, are located near major rivers or lakes. Hence urban areas should generate substantial amounts of traceable permit activity. This should be evident, especially in water-quality laws such as the Inland Lakes and Streams Act, since all activities in or near rivers and floodplains are regulated by these acts. Yet the analysis showed that all major developed areas had a negative correlation with the regulatory activities of the Department of Natural Resources.

The reason for the reduction in environmental regulatory activities by the Land and Water Management Division in the urban areas is not totally clear. One explanation is that larger cities through zoning and city codes regulate their own water quality and related land use. This focuses the attention of state environmental statutes on the rural areas. Through this disparity in the regulatory system, the larger metropolitan areas emerge independent from the state environmental regulations.

Black has argued that "law is greater in a direction toward less culture than toward more culture."[21] The regional concentrations of social and economic variables defining cultural complexity clearly support the theory that environmental law is less intensively enforced in areas with more cultural activities. Economides, Blacksell, and Watkins have commented that

> If Black's theory could be validated . . . and some of the empirical techniques evolved by geographers might help here, then it would provide a basis for elucidating the enigmatic triangular relationship between law, territory and social space. Such a development could alter fundamentally the traditional, rigid, positivist view of distance which has been incorporated previously into much social theory.[22]

The results of the research presented in this chapter provide evidence of the "enigmatic triangular relationship between law, territory and social space." Because such research focuses on environmental law rather than law in general, the distinction between the geographic location of social space and the physical nature of the territory becomes more important. This research suggests that environmental law is aimed at undeveloped areas rather than developed areas. Rather than human activities, it is the physical nature of an area that appears to determine the regional efficacy of environmental law. This drastically reduces the spatial flexibility of environmental law in Michigan.

NOTES

1. Stanley D. Brunn (1974), *Geography and Politics in America* (New York: Harper and Row); Keith D. Harries and Stanley D. Brunn (1978), *The Geography of Laws and Justice: Spatial Perspectives on the Criminal Justice System* (New York: Praeger); Rutherford H. Platt (1976), *Land Use Control: Interface of Law and Geography* (Washington, D.C.: Association of American Geographers).

2. Mark Blacksell (1986), "Human Geography and Law: A Case of Separate Development in Social Science," *Progress in Human Geography,* 10, pp. 371–396.

3. Michael Dear and Gordon L. Clark (1981), "Dimensions of Local State Autonomy," *Environment and Planning,* A, 13, pp. 1277–1294; Gordon L. Clark (1981), "Law,

the State and the Spatial Integration of the United States," *Environment and Planning,* A, 13, pp. 1197–1232; R. J. Johnston (1981), "The Management and Autonomy of the Local State: The Role of the Judiciary in the United States," *Environment and Planning,* A, 13, pp. 1305–1315.

4.   Gordon H. Pirie (1983), "On Spatial Justice," *Environment and Planning,* A, 15, pp. 465–473; David R. Reynolds and Fred M. Shelley (1985), "Procedural Justice and Local Democracy," *Political Geography Quarterly,* 4, pp. 267–288.

5.   Derwent Whittlesey (1939), *The Earth and the State.* New York: Henry Holt, p. 588.

6.   Environmental Protection Act of 1970, Michigan Compiled Laws Annotated §§691.1201–1207 (West Supp. 1984).

7.   Daniel K. Slone (1985), "The Michigan Environmental Protection Act: Bringing Citizen-Initiated Environmental Suits Into the 1980s," *Ecology Law Quarterly,* 12, pp. 271–362.

8.   Leslie B. Curzon (1979), *Jurisprudence.* Plymouth: Macdonald and Evans, p. 7.

9.   *Ibid.,* pp. 9–10.

10.   John H. Wigmore (1929), *A Panorama of the World's Legal Systems.* St. Paul, Minn.: West Publishing Company.

11.   Bronislaw Malinowski (1945), *The Dynamics of Culture Change* (New Haven: Yale University Press); Bronislaw Malinowski (1966), *Crime and Custom in Savage Society,* 8th edition (London: Routledge and Kegan Paul); Edward A. Hoebel (1954), *The Law of Primitive Man: A Study in Comparative Legal Systems* (Cambridge: Harvard University Press); Laura Nader and Harry F. Todd Jr. (1978), *The Disputing Process — Law in Ten Societies* (New York: Columbia University Press).

12.   J. Van Velsen (1969), "Procedural Informality, Reconciliation and False Comparisons," in *Ideas and Procedures in African Customary Law,* edited by M. Gluckman. London: Oxford University Press.

13.   William Pattison (1979), *The Beginnings of the American Rectangular Land Survey System.* New York: Arno Press.

14.   Norman J.W. Thrower (1966), *Original Survey and Land Subdivision.* Washington, D.C.: Association of American Geographers.

15.   Wigmore, (1929), op. cit.; Ernest S. Easterly III (1977), "Global Patterns of Legal Systems: Notes Toward a New Geojurisprudence," *Geographical Review,* 67, pp. 209–220.

16.   Gerald J. Postema (1986), *Bentham and the Common Law Tradition.* Oxford: Clarendon Press, p. 66.

17.   Jeroen Wagendorp (1984), "Inland Seawalls in Southwestern Michigan: A Limnological Approach," M. A. thesis, Department of Geography, Western Michigan University, Kalamazoo. For a detailed account of the methods and findings (and for maps of the regions), see Jeroen Wagendorp, "The Regional Efficacy of Environmental Law in Michigan," Ph.D. dissertation, University of Oklahoma, 1989.

18. Michigan Inland Lakes and Streams Act, Michigan Compiled Laws Annotated §§281.951–965 (West 1979); Flood, Drainage and Beach Erosion Act, Michigan Compiled Laws Annotated §§281.621–628 (West 1979); Soil Erosion and Sedimentation Control Act of 1972, Michigan Compiled Laws Annotated §§282.101–117 (West 1979); Goemaere-Anderson Wetlands Protection Act, Michigan Compiled Laws Annotated §§281.701–722 (West Supp. 1984).

19. Great Lakes Submerged Lands Act, Michigan Compiled Laws Annotated §§322.701–715 (West 1979).

20. G. Sheppard (1971), "Milliken Promises Zoning to Save the North," *North Woods Call,* June 23, p. 3.

21. Donald L. Black (1976), *The Behavior of Law.* New York: Academic Press.

22. Kim Economides, Mark Blacksell, and Charles Watkins (1986), "The Spatial Analysis of Legal Systems: Toward a Geography of Law," *Journal of Law and Society,* 13, pp. 161–182.

9
REFLECTIONS ON THE FUTURE

GARY L. THOMPSON, FRED M. SHELLEY, AND CHAND WIJE

Authors of the previous chapters have addressed interactions between geography and environmental law in the United States from a variety of perspectives. Case studies of water law, minerals, forensic geography, and land use laws illustrate the extent to which laws are shaped by and in turn influence geography, informing both intellectual traditions. Geographers examining environmental questions have become increasingly aware of the role of law and the legal system in resolving environmental conflicts, while students and practitioners of the law have become more and more knowledgeable about the role of place, location, and context in the development, application, and effectiveness of laws and legislative efforts.

In this concluding chapter, we build upon the contributions made by the individual chapter authors in order to address two critical questions. First, what are the important social forces that can be expected to shape the interface between geography and environmental law in the years ahead? In what ways can we expect such changes to influence the developing relationships between law and geography? Second, how might such developments affect a research agenda involving geography and environmental law? More generally, what research questions do the chapters in this volume and other analyses of interaction between law and geography suggest, and how might these questions be addressed fruitfully and effectively?

In addressing these questions, we develop three basic themes. These include the end of the cold war and the consequent emphasis on international trade within a restructured global economy, the effect of changes in American domestic politics on environmental legislation, and the potential role of geographic information systems and other new technologies in enhancing the interface between geography and American environmental law. The concluding section briefly sketches possible research agendas for future investigation into the law–geography interface.

THE NEW WORLD ORDER, GEOGRAPHY, AND ENVIRONMENTAL LAW

Both law and geography change in response to societal and technological developments as well as the results of scientific inquiry. The contemporary world is one of unprecedented change, and we can assume that both environmental law and geographical inquiry will evolve in correspondingly dramatic fashion. What, then, are the major changes that we can expect? How might these influence laws, geographies, and the relationships between them?

Perhaps the most significant development of recent years has been the collapse of Soviet communism and the end of the cold war. For nearly half a century, American political and economic life was dominated by the cold war. The cold war was much more than ongoing competition between East and West; it was also a world order, a filter through which Americans and others viewed the world.

The cold war came to an abrupt end in the late 1980s, as communist dictatorships in Eastern Europe collapsed and were replaced by freely elected governments. The Berlin Wall — that symbol of the Iron Curtain that had descended across the European continent after World War II — was torn down. In 1990, East and West Germany reunified. The following year the Soviet government itself collapsed. The former Soviet republics became independent countries, and many struggled in the process of transition between dictatorship and democracy and between planned and market economies.

With the end of the cold war has come the end of the cold war world order. In its place a much different global structure is evolving. No doubt some common means of looking at the world will eventually emerge, yet as of the mid–1990s there were no clear indications about its characteristics or impacts on American society. In the past, transitions between geopolitical orders have been more abrupt, with world orders dominant for only a generation or so.[1] The mid-1940s, when the pre–World War II, European-centered international system gave way to the cold war, was one such transition period.[2] Our current transition period will undoubtedly afford future historians a wealth of opportunities to interpret significant events of the present day.

To what extent might the interface between geography and environmental law be shaped by the developing world order? Many have speculated that the new world order will be influenced much more significantly by global economic changes and international trade than had been the case in the past. To the extent that this prediction proves true, it is likely that those who create future environmental laws as well as modifications to existing laws will consider their actual or potential effects on patterns of global trade and exchange within the world economy.

This could affect environmental law in several ways. First, we can expect more coordination between the United States and other countries concerning environmental regulation. Vice President Al Gore has argued, in fact, that concern for the global environment is likely to be a major aspect of the emerging new world order itself.[3] Second, it is likely that the volume of international trade in resources and other environmentally sensitive products will increase as trade barriers between former enemies are lifted. For example, the considerable oil and gas reserves of the former Soviet Union may now become accessible to American oil companies, which will have a significant impact on both the pattern of international petroleum trade and the development of environmental laws affecting petroleum production and utilization.

Certainly, we can expect that the development of new environmental laws will be increasingly influenced by international considerations. During the 1980s the United States became involved in several controversies with other countries concerning the enactment or enforcement of environmental laws. These included ongoing disputes with Japan over whaling and the use of fishing technologies believed to endanger marine mammals and disagreement with the European Community concerning the importation of steroid-fed American beef cattle across the Atlantic.

In November 1994 the United States ratified the revised General Agreement on Tariffs and Trade (GATT), an international treaty designed to promote free trade by reducing or removing trade barriers among its members. Previous versions of GATT had failed to come to grips with environmental issues. The revised GATT treaty, which calls for the establishment of an agency to be known as the World Trade Organization, is much more explicit in linking trade to environmental considerations. Thus legislators will likely begin to pay careful attention to the mutual effects of environmental legislation and international trade. For example, American exports of cigarettes, baby formula, pesticides, chemicals, and other goods held responsible for health or environmental damages may be limited or regulated under the auspices of the new World Trade Organization.

Along the same lines, we can expect that the United States and other countries will undertake more concerted efforts to coordinate environmental policy. The Montreal Protocol on ozone-creating fluorocarbons is an example. Some have charged that global production is moving into less-developed countries in order to avoid the increased production costs associated with the stronger environmental protection laws characteristic of the United States and other developed countries. Developed countries will have to ascertain that international competition for scarce economic resources does not imply competition among countries to weaken environmental standards, to the long-run detriment of the environment.

Such changes are likely as well in accordance with improved understanding of the global environment. Scientists have become increasingly aware that the complexities of the global environment transcend international boundaries. For example, biologists are only beginning to understand the effects of rainforest depletion on population dynamics of migratory birds that breed in North America. Some in fact believe that many bird species that breed in North America and spend the winter in Mexico, Central America, or South America are becoming endangered because their winter habitat has been destroyed as a result of deforestation.[4] Likewise, climatologists are only starting to understand global atmospheric circulation patterns. Scientists are investigating the effects of phenomena such as El Niño on weather patterns worldwide and are studying how the "holes" in the earth's ozone layer affect ultraviolet radiation, global warming, and sea-level rise. As our understanding of these and other aspects of global climate becomes more sophisticated, we can put this knowledge to use in modifying and improving environmental law in the United States and other countries.

Another area of interface between geography and international environmental law involves the law of the sea. Following years of controversy during the height of the cold war, the international community developed a Law of the Sea treaty to provide for common international management of the physical and biotic resources of the world's oceans. The United States and several other industrialized countries objected to the treaty's emphasis on international management of minerals and other seabed resources and refused to sign the treaty. In the early 1990s, the treaty was revised in order to address American objections, and President Bill Clinton signed the revised treaty in 1994. The revised Law of the Sea treaty stipulates international cooperation in managing the ocean's resources for the common benefit of people throughout the world.

Geographers have long been active in research involving the ocean and its resources, management, and legal status.[5] Many contributions to the voluminous literature concerning the negotiations, ratification, and actual and potential impacts of the Law of the Sea treaty have been written from an explicitly geographical perspective.[6] American participation in the Law of the Sea treaty will undoubtedly provide opportunities for cooperation between geographers and lawyers in the areas of boundary delineation, resource management, transportation, and many other fields of interest to both disciplines.

THE CHANGING DOMESTIC POLITICAL SITUATION

On November 8, 1994, the American electorate dealt the incumbent administration of Democratic president Bill Clinton a stunning rebuke. As a result, for the first time since the 1950s, both houses of Congress had Republican majorities. How might the election of 1994 — and the potentially dramatic shift in voter opinion concerning the role of governance in society that it represents — affect geography and environmental law?

Environmental issues have played a prominent role in the American political agenda since World War II. Evidence of extensive air and water pollution in industrial areas led many to advocate an expanded federal role in solving environmental problems. Since that time geographic patterns of support and opposition to environmental proposals have closely followed changes in the White House.[7]

By the late 1950s, support for increased federal funding for pollution control and other environmental legislation had become associated with the Democratic Party. Indeed, there is considerable evidence that the Democrats used pollution control as an issue to shore up support among blue-collar workers in the late 1950s.[8] In 1959 President Dwight D. Eisenhower vetoed a bill intended to expand federal support of state and local pollution control projects on the grounds that the bill was too expensive and would erode local responsibility for what the president regarded as a local problem. An attempt on the part of Democrats in Congress to override the president's veto failed in early 1960, with most members of Congress voting along party lines.[9]

During the 1960s, the environment became an increasingly important public issue. Books such as *The Quiet Crisis* by Interior Secretary Stewart Udall and *Silent Spring* by Rachel Carson were influential in raising the awareness of ordinary Americans concerning environmental problems.[10] As time went on, however, the Democrats became identified as the pro-environment party, and the Republicans were seen as opposing strong environmental protection laws. Yet organizations such as the Environmental Protection Agency (EPA) were established and many of the major environmental laws still in force today, including the Clean Water Act of 1972 and the Endangered Species Act of 1973, were enacted during the Republican administration of Richard Nixon, who supported strong environmental policies in order to placate opposition to his Vietnam War policies among younger voters, liberals, and moderates.[11] By the late 1970s, Congress had become more and more polarized between Democratic supporters and Republican opponents of strong environmental laws, with this distinction remaining in effect today. Many Republicans objected, in fact, to the environmentally oriented positions espoused by the Clinton appointees who served as American delegates to the United Nations conference on environment and development in Rio de Janeiro in the summer of 1994.

By the 1990s surveys indicated that the American electorate was increasingly disenchanted with the size and scope of the federal government, despite Clinton's 1992 defeat of Republican president George Bush. In 1994 Republicans throughout the United States campaigned not only against an unpopular Democratic president but also against a federal bureaucracy that many had come to regard as intrusive and unmanageable. The leadership of the new Republican Congress promised far-reaching and dramatic action to reverse the general trend toward expanded federal influence in American life — a trend identified more and more with the Democratic Party in earlier decades. It is expected that the

Republican leadership will act to promote increased individual, state, and local responsibility for environmental and other problems.

Republican criticism of and opposition to the size, power, and influence of the federal government may thus result in the weakening or elimination of environmental laws, especially at the federal level. For example, some members of Congress have already called for the repeal or modification of the Endangered Species Act. Others have proposed that federal standards for clean air and water be weakened and that responsibility for environmental protection be shifted from the federal government to the states. Many critics have pointed out that the very process of regulation associated with federal bureaucracy has made the situation worse than had been the case prior to the establishment of regulatory authority. For example, critics have charged that not only the EPA but other regulatory agencies such as the Food and Drug Administration are so inefficient and corrupt that they create problems far more significant than those they were established to address.

What will happen if regulatory agencies are dismantled or weakened? It is possible that this would enhance the authority of powerful local economic interests. The permitting process associated with mineral resource development described in Chapter 6, for example, may be reduced in length and complexity in order to encourage rather than restrict mineral exploration. Likewise, the domination of environmental policy by highly populated and economically powerful interests within states such as Michigan, as discussed in Chapter 8, may be reinforced by a curtailed federal role in environmental policy.

Proponents of strong environmental laws may be heartened, however, by evidence that levels of support for environmental protection among Americans of all political persuasions have increased steadily since the 1970s.[12] In 1980 Republican Ronald Reagan, running on a conservative platform, defeated incumbent Democrat President Jimmy Carter in a landslide. Reagan's popularity was instrumental in giving the Republicans a majority in the Senate — a majority that they held for six years. Yet efforts on the part of Reagan and some of his conservative supporters to repeal environmental proposals of previous administrations were rebuffed, and controversial appointees such as Secretary of the Interior James Watt and EPA administrator Anne Gorsuch Burford were subject to widespread criticism and eventually forced to leave office. By the late 1980s, Republicans as well as Democrats had become aware of public opinion and took stronger environmentalist positions. Although perceptions of the responsibility for the environment may shift dramatically in the years ahead, it is unlikely that the American electorate will accept wholesale elimination of governmental protection of the environment. Indeed, it is entirely possible that the regulatory process may be more successful if undertaken at the state and local levels.

GEOGRAPHIC INFORMATION SYSTEMS AND ENVIRONMENTAL LAW

While societal changes such as the end of the cold war, the expansion of international trade, and rising frustration with the federal bureaucracy will undoubtedly affect the relationships between geography and American environmental law in the future, these relationships will also be influenced by changes within the discipline of geography itself. In recent years the use of geographic information systems and other research techniques has had a dramatic impact on the process of geographical research — a process that will help determine how geographers examine environmental law and its effects on society in the years ahead.

Geographic information systems are computer software packages that can simultaneously organize, analyze, and display geographically disaggregated data. Geographic information systems include three primary components: data storage capability, statistical analysis capability, and mapping capability. In most geographic information systems, data are arranged in matrix form. Each row of the matrix represents a place, and each column includes variables measured by place and in some circumstances over time.

Geographic information systems have contributed to the process of geographic research in a variety of ways. Their flexibility in organizing and presenting geographically disaggregated data has dramatically reduced the cost and effort associated with map production. As we have seen, many of the various aspects of environmental law considered from a geographical perspective in this volume involve extensive use of maps. For example, the discussion in Chapter 7 on determining riparian and marine boundaries indicates the importance of matching historical accounts of boundaries and landscape features with the location of these features on the earth's surface today. Such a matchup will be greatly expedited through the use of geographic information systems.

Many different types of maps can be produced, including maps of individual variables, new variables created by combining original ones, and the results of statistical analyses. Many geographic information systems are interactive, enabling the researcher to visualize relationships within data matrices while creating new variables by manipulating existing variables. For example, a researcher interested in patterns of land use near floodplains or earthquake faults — following the discussion in Chapters 1 and 5 can interact with the geographic information system by mapping floodplains or faults and calculating population densities, land values, or other critical variables within specified distances of the natural hazards in question. Thus geographic information systems technology combines communication with research capability.

Since the late 1980s, the use of geographic information systems in academic research, business and industry, planning, government, and other contexts has risen dramatically. Experts in the industry have in fact predicted that more than half a million geographic information systems will be in use throughout the world by 2000.[13] Such systems can influence the interface between geography and environmental law in several ways. As we have seen, they have revolutionized geographical research dramatically by integrating three of geography's traditional functions — cartography, data management, and data analysis.

In addition, it is entirely possible that geographic information systems technology may enter the courtroom. For example, could geographic information systems be used to predict whether mining in a particular area could have a long-run deleterious impact on vegetation or animal life in a wilderness region? Might courts base decisions on whether to permit mining in such areas based on predictions such as these? Another potential effect of geographical information systems is in tracing the impact of past land use decisions on present and future environments. For example, Terry has developed a method to use geographic information systems to examine changes in land use associated with oil-field development and applied this procedure to categorizing changes in land use in the Healdton, Oklahoma, oil field.[14] Geographers with training in geographic information systems will have much to offer those who practice environmental law in legislatures and courtrooms.

CONCLUSION

During the final decade of the twentieth century, we have witnessed several important developments that are likely to enhance and restructure the already substantial interface between geography and environmental law. The end of the cold war has generated a new world order that will probably emphasize international trade. At the same time, the American electorate is increasingly rejecting big government and bureaucracy in favor of local management of local problems. Meanwhile, the development of geographical information systems has revolutionized the process of geographical research, greatly improving the range and flexibility of geographical data analysis of interest to the legal profession.

How might these and related developments contribute to an agenda for further research on geography and American environmental law? Geographic information systems can be used to improve the categorization of places for legal purposes. Many environmental laws divide places into categories — for example laws regarding wilderness use identify criteria to determine the degree of legal protection required, while streams, watersheds, and airsheds are categorized according to levels of present and potential pollution. At times, critics have charged that the designation of specific wilderness areas, streams, and other areas into particular categories is arbitrary or informed by politics rather than by accurate geographical knowledge. Both the classification process and the development of classification schemes themselves can be enhanced by the use of geographic information systems.

Geographic information systems and other technological advances in the process of geographical research can also help in predicting the consequences of environmental laws. As is evident throughout this book, geographers are only beginning to grasp the complexity of the global physical environment and its integration into the world economy. History is replete with examples of laws that proved inappropriate for the environments to which they were applied. As Chapter 4 indicated, for example, the riparian principle of water law developed in England was not germane to the western United States, where it was replaced by the appropriation principle. Many of the problems associated with Texas groundwater law today have come about because that law is based on the riparian principle and fails to recognize the linkages between groundwater and other aspects of the hydrologic cycle.

In the contemporary world, geographical knowledge can and should continue to inform proposals to regulate and manage land use and the environment. The geographer's knowledge of how people perceive, use, and treat the physical environment can and should play an even more central role in the process of preparing environmental law than is presently the case. What is needed is more geographical research and more integration of the results of this research into the legal process. It is hoped that the chapters in this volume will represent a first positive step in that direction.

NOTES

1.   Peter J. Taylor (ed.) (1990), *Political Geography of the Twentieth Century: A Global Analysis.* London: Belhaven.

2.   Peter J. Taylor (1993), *Britain and the Cold War.* New York: Guilford.

3.   Albert Gore Jr. (1992), *Earth in the Balance.* Boston: Houghton Mifflin.

4.   John Terborgh (1989), *Where Have All the Birds Gone? Essays on the Biology and Conservation of Birds That Migrate to the American Tropics.* Princeton: Princeton University Press.

5.   S. Whittemore Boggs (1951), "National Claims in Adjacent Seas," *Geographical Review,* 41, pp. 185–209; S. Whittemore Boggs (1951), "Delimitation of Seaward Areas Under National Jurisdiction," *American Journal of International Law,* 45, pp. 240–266; G. Etzel Pearcy (1959), "Geographical Aspects of the Law of the Sea," *Annals,* Association of American Geographers, 49, pp. 1–23; Lewis M. Alexander (1968), "Geography and the Law of the Sea," *Annals,* Association of American Geographers, 58, pp. 177–197.

6.   Mark B. Feldman and David Colson (1981), "The Maritime Boundaries of the United States," *American Journal of International Law,* 77, pp. 219–238; Lewis M. Alexander (1986), "The Delimitation of Maritime Boundaries," *Political Geography Quarterly,* 5, pp. 19–24; Martin Glassner, "The Frontiers of Earth — and of Political Geography: The Sea, Antarctica and Outer Space," *Political Geography Quarterly,* 10, pp. 422–437.

7.   Fred M. Shelley (1995), "The Changing Geographic Pattern of Support for Environmental Legislation in the House of Representatives, 1971–1989," *Environmental History Review.*

8.   William D. Solecki and Fred M. Shelley (1995), "The Role of Environmental Issues in the Restructuring of American Politics in the Late 1950s," paper presented to the annual meeting of the American Society for Environmental History, Las Vegas, Nevada.

9.   *Congressional Record,* February 15, 1960.

10.   Stewart Udall (1963), *The Quiet Crisis* (New York: Holt, Rinehart and Winston); Rachel Carson (1962), *Silent Spring* (Boston: Houghton Mifflin).

11.   Tom Wicker (1991), *One of Us: Richard Nixon and the American Dream.* New York: Random House.

12.   Samuel P. Hays (1989), *Beauty, Health and Permanence: Environmental Politics in the United States, 1955–1985.* New York: Cambridge University Press.

13.   David Green, David Rix, and James Cadoux-Hudson (1994), *Geographic Information 1994.* London: Taylor and Francis.

14.   Sean P. Terry (1995), "Land Use Changes in the Healdton, Oklahoma Oil Field," Ph.D. dissertation, Department of Geography, University of Oklahoma, Norman.

INDEX